Musings of the Man in the Cave

REVISED EDITION

Dennis Binns

Writers Apex

Gateway Towards Success

8063 MADISON AVE #1252
Indianapolis, IN 46227
+13176596889
www.writersapex.com

PRAYERS

PONDERINGS

POEMS

QUOTES

Great Spirit, Almighty Healer, and Creator of all things, it is with a humble heart that we congregate to offer our thankfulness. We thank you for the sacred circles found throughout your creation, from the ever-expanding universe to the nests of the birds that surround us. We thank you for the seasonal circles that remind us of rejuvenation, regrowth, harvest, and repose within the cycle. We thank you for the music found in the winds and the rushing waters. We thank you for our earth as it supplies us with all we need to survive. For the wildflowers in the summer to the falling snow of the winter, we thank you. We thank you for calming waters and crashing shorelines. We thank you for the towering trees of the forests. We thank you for the many herbs that provide cures for our ailments.

We ask for comfort for those that have lost loved ones. We ask for greater charity toward the poor, widows, and homeless. May we think of them each winter. We ask for strength, courage, and guidance for those that are now meeting their ancestors and loved ones in the Spirit World. We ask for the cures for all diseases, ailments, pestilences, and disorders that come forth. For those that are low in spirit, we ask for their comfort and guidance. We ask for an era of peace and true equality, where no one person has more power than the next. We ask for the return of our abducted sons and daughters and protect them from harm. We ask for guidance as we continue along our paths, so we choose the right direction. We ask for a greater awakening and a cleansing of our spirits to prepare us for the arduous task of rebalancing that lies ahead. We ask for protection against the onslaught of evil that tends to run unabashed throughout the world.

We look to your compassion for the answering of our prayers. We understand that you have granted us the knowledge that you are in control of all things, though we may not understand why or how certain things happen. You have blessed us with the Sacred Spirit that resides within us, to guide us along our path. You have opened the veil of secrets that have brought forth new friends and family that bring us the insight we need, handed out in portions, as we continue our journey. We look forward to new adventures along life's path. So, it is. So shall it be.

reat Spirit, Almighty Healer, and Creator of all things, it is with humble hearts that we congregate to offer up requests alongside our deepest gratitude. We thank you for the season of renewal when new life is formed. We thank you for the season of growth where planted seeds have reached their optimum growth. We thank you for the season of harvest with its woodland covering of diverse colored leaves. We thank you for the season of slumber that Mother Earth uses to rest and prepare for the next cycle.

We ask for a return to the ancient days while life was innocent and according to your purpose. We ask for an end to the dark forces that have enslaved your children for too long. We ask for truth to find its way once again into the minds of those of us that remain during this transition. We ask for an end to fear that has kept us down. We ask for a new beginning where we are guided on the right path. We ask that the proud become humbled; the hateful become more loving; the hoarders become more giving. We ask for an end to the unlawful taxation that has served to keep us too busy to ask questions. We ask for what is rightfully ours and to return us to a place of prominence and prosperity. We ask for an end to the lawlessness. We ask for a righting of the ship where things become as they were in the beginning before Adam and Eve listened to the reptile. We ask for an end to homelessness. For those that need healing of their afflictions of the mind, body, or spirit, we ask for that to be granted.

We thank you for the guidance you send so we may follow our path with strong legs and straight eyes. We thank you for our elders that have given us tools we need along our journey. We thank you for our children that will carry the lessons and wisdom on to the next generation. We thank you for our thorns that keep us from becoming too proud or boastful. We thank you for the music that accompanies the coolness of the evening air. We thank you for the vastness of the universe that surrounds us and all the mysteries it holds. So it is, so shall it be.

G reat Spirit, Almighty Healer, and Creator of all things, it is with humble hearts that we gather to offer many thanks. We thank you for all the two-legged, four-legged, swimmers, fliers, and crawlers. We thank you for the rocks, clay, sand, soil, and the uniqueness of each. We thank you for the sacredness of all life. We thank you for the forests, jungles, plains, deserts, and ice caps. We thank you for the waters that flow from the snow-capped peaks cascading down around the rocks and waterfalls, to the rivers and lakes below. We thank you for the gentle breezes that caress our skin and bring calmness to our spirit. We thank you for the air we breathe, food we eat, and waters that hydrate all living things.

We ask for guidance to be granted to our leaders during this turbulent time. May they choose carefully during the decision-making processes. We ask for your healing hands to be placed upon those that are suffering through afflictions of the spirit, body, or mind. For those that have lost loved ones, we ask for your comfort to be granted to them during the grieving process. We ask for mercy toward those that have no regard for the sanctity of life. May they learn that all life is given as a gift, and each is sacred. We ask for an end to the abduction and murders of our women and children. We ask for mercy for those that continue to follow you even in our darkest hours. We ask for a greater awakening for those whose hearts remain dormant. We ask for guidance each day for all that continue with love and compassion in their heart. We ask for an era of peace and tranquility, where true equality among your children is shown throughout the four corners. We ask for a time of rest, so our Earth Mother is allowed to regenerate nature to where it was in the beginning. We ask for honor and integrity to once again enter into the hearts of our leaders.

We thank you for family and friends that have given us the support we need along our journey. We thank you for our elders that give us the stories, wisdom, and instruction needed each day. We thank you for our children that have reminded us of the innocence we have long forgotten. We thank you for those that come to us for a short time, to provide us with the insight we need to overcome our obstacles. We thank you for our trials that serve to strengthen and prepare us for that which lies ahead. We thank you for our thorns that prevent us from becoming boastful and proud. So, it is. So shall it be.

Great Spirit, Almighty Healer, and Creator of all things, it is with humble hearts that we unify, as one, to offer our gratitude. We thank you for all that our eyes can see, from the mountaintops to the oceans; the differing dimensions; and the third heaven where your throne resides. We thank you for the vastness of the universe that surrounds us. We thank you for the unique gifts that you have blessed us with. May we use them, through your guidance, for the benefit of all living things. We thank you for the many blessings you have bestowed upon your children. We thank you for our elders that prepare us for that which lies ahead. We thank you for our ancestors whose words of wisdom have been passed on from one generation to the next. We thank you for our children who will one day pass on all they have learned onto the next generation.

We ask for your guidance as many begin their journeys throughout many lands. We ask for your protection, strength and blessings as we begin to embark to protect the animals, bring food to the inhabitants of the forests, assist those in need along our path. We ask for protection, strength and guidance for those that continue to stand against the environmental onslaught perpetrated by an uncaring society. We ask for strength, guidance, and discernment to further the cause of righteousness in our country and its governance. We ask for great healing this year of change for those that are suffering spiritually, physically, and mentally. We ask that you bring strength and comfort during their healing process. We ask for the release of all political prisoners being held without just cause. We ask for an end to all forms of violence and that your truth and justice prevails.

We understand the necessity of refocusing our attention to you instead of the world, building our faith, and acknowledging that you are always in firm control. We strongly believe in your omnipotence and compassion for all your creation. We give worship and praise to your right-ruling and mercy. So, it is. So shall it be.

reat Spirit, Almighty Healer, and Creator of all things, it is with
humble hearts that we gather, as one, to offer many thanks for all
that you have provided. We thank you for the songs of the wrens in
the early morning hours. We thank you for the diverse colors of the wildflowers
along the plains. We thank you for the early morning breeze as it gently caresses
our cheeks. We thank you for the beauty of the butterfly as it emerges from its
cocoon. We thank you for the strength of the sycamore and redwood, as they
stretch out to the heavens. We thank you for the beauty of the oak, maple, and
birch during the autumn months.

We ask for rain to come to those areas of drought, and where there may be
fires that endanger lives. We have done much to bring displeasure to you over
the centuries. We have brought destruction to the lands through our mining,
fracking and drilling; littered our lands; polluted our air and waterways. We ask
for your forgiveness. May we return to a time where we were better caretakers of
all you have created. We have not properly cared for the animals as we should. We
have hunted for sport and trophies, rather than for necessity. Again, we ask for
your forgiveness. We ask for your guidance as we return our focus back to you,
rather than continue the destructive ways of the world. We ask for transparency
in the halls of our government and to end the corruption throughout the country.
We ask for the release of all political prisoners incarcerated over crimes they did
not commit. We ask for an end to the violence the permeates throughout the
four corners. We ask for the strengthening of our indigenous cultures. May we
take a pause and finally listen to the words they speak.

We thank you for rainforests that provide us with air we breathe. We thank you
for the calmness of the waters in the early morning hours. We thank you for
the four seasons that remind us of the cycle of life. We thank you for your love,
discipline, forgiveness and blessings. May we bring honor and humility back into
a world that has fixated itself on selfishness and arrogance. We thank you for all
answered prayers. So, it is. So shall it be.

Great Spirit, Almighty Healer, and Creator of all things, it is with a humble heart that we unite to offer many thanks. We thank you for the small birds in the nest. We thank you for the diversity of the fish in the seas. We thank you for the crab as it scampers about the rocks on the shore. We thank you for the calmness of the waters in the early morning hours. For the trees that give us the oxygen, from the carbon dioxide, that allows us to breathe, we thank you. We thank you for the clouds that bring the rain to areas of need.

We have transgressed much against you and ask for your forgiveness. We ask that your chosen people recognize the sign in the heavens, as it appears over your holy land, and understand its meaning. We ask for truth to prevail over the deception that has permeated throughout the centuries. We ask for calmness and tranquility in a world of chaos and destruction. We ask that the veil be pulled further apart so all may see more that has been hidden. We ask for patience when we tend to do things ourselves, rather than awaiting your time of accomplishment. We ask for mercy, Father, for those times we have forgotten to focus upon you, instead of the world around us. We ask for love, where there is hatred; peace, where there is conflict; understanding, where there is confusion; and transparency, where there is deception. We ask for miracles for those that are despondent and searching for relief. We ask for healing for those that are suffering through diverse diseases, disorders, and ailments.

We thank you for the ocean waves that gracefully stretch upon the sandy shore. We thank you for the cool gentle breeze as it softly caresses our skin. We thank you for the beauty of the whale and dolphin as they break the surface of the ocean waters. We thank you for all four legged, two legged, swimmers, fliers, and crawlers that inhabit Mother Earth. We thank you for your forgiveness, love, patience, and blessings that you have provided us. So, it is. So shall it be.

Great Spirit, Almighty Healer, and Creator of all things, it is with a humble heart that we gather to offer many thanks. We thank you for the rains that come to areas of great thirst. We thank you for the seasonal cycles that remind us of rejuvenation, growth, and rest within the circle. We thank you for the music found in the winds and the rushing waters. We thank you for Mother Earth as she supplies us with all we need to survive. We thank you for the lifeblood of all living things. We thank you for all the mysteries of the universe we behold. We thank you for the music we find in the early morning hours, as the songbirds begin their songs.

We ask for strength, courage, and guidance for those that are now meeting their ancestors and loved ones in the Spirit World. We ask for miraculous healing for those that are suffering from afflictions of the spirit, mind, or body. For those that are low in spirit, we ask for their comfort and guidance. We ask for protection, courage, and strength for all that will stand against the onslaught of destruction to our environment, and animals by those that do not understand what they are doing. We ask for an end to the hatred that seeks to divide your people. We ask for an end to the greed and lust of power that seeks to destroy the spirits of many. We ask for an era of peace and true equality, where no one person has more power than the next. We ask for the return of our abducted sons and daughters and protect them from harm. We ask for guidance as we continue along our paths, so we may choose the right direction. We ask for freedom for those that continue to suffer incarceration for crimes they did not commit. We ask for greater compassion to soften the hardened hearts who do not understand the suffering of the homeless and the poor. We ask for a bountiful harvest, so we may provide food for those that are starving throughout all four corners. We ask for a greater awakening and a cleansing of our spirits to prepare us for the arduous task of rebalancing that lies ahead. We ask for protection of our animal friends that are facing grave danger from those that would kill them for trophies. We ask for forgiveness, our country is divided by two factions, one for trying to bring your laws back into our lives, and the other for continuing to keep them out. We ask for your mercy, Father, as we begin to stand up for what is righteous.

We thank you for all the two-legged, four-legged, swimmers, fliers and crawlers that interact with us and bring us insight and wisdom. We thank you for the strength of the wisdom that lies within our hearts. We thank you for the many trials we endure so they may strengthen our spirit and prepare us for the future. So, it is. So shall it be.

reat Spirit, Almighty Healer, and Creator of all things, it is with
humble hearts that we gather this day to offer up the many thanks you
so deserve. We give thanks for our daily food and ask for its blessing.
We give thanks for the waters from the snow-capped mountains, that cascade
down to the lakes and oceans below, in which can hydrate the bodies of all living
things. We give thanks for the gentleness of the early morning breeze, as the sun
rises to bring warmth and growth. We give thanks for the flight of the many
fliers throughout the four corners. We give thanks for those times, when we are
in nature, understanding that all living things, from the plants to the animals,
need pure water to survive.

We give thanks for all two-legged, four-legged, swimmers, fliers and crawlers
upon the lands. We give thanks for the air we receive from the trees, as we give
them the carbon dioxide they need. We give thanks for the beauty of the butterfly
emerging from the cocoon to the hummingbird as it hovers to receive his nectar.
We give thanks for the bees that pollinate the plants and assist in bringing us a
healthy environment. We give thanks for the ants that work tirelessly to aerate
the soil each day. For the warmth of the summer to the coolness of the winter, we
give thanks. We give thanks for fields of grain that will feed the people across the
great waters, as well as here in our homeland. We give thanks for the multitudes
and diverseness of the swimmers in the ocean waters. We give thanks for the
oak, birch, and maple leaves in magnificent colors during the autumn season,
as well as the soft snow flurries of the winter months.

We give thanks for the knowledge you allow us to receive, so we may marvel at
the perfection of your creation. We give thanks for the stars above that we may
see the signs given to us. We give thanks for our elders and our children. We
give thanks for family and friends that support and defend us. We give thanks
for those that serve to keep us safe. So, it is. So shall it be.

Great Spirit, Almighty Healer, and Creator of all things, it is with a humble heart that we gather to offer many thanks. We thank you for the many gifts and blessings that you have bestowed upon your children. May we use them for the betterment of all. We thank you for our trials that help to strengthen our spirits. We thank you for our elders and the life lessons they have given us to assist us on our journey. We thank you for our children that will take these lessons and build upon the unbreakable foundation this generation will leave them.

We ask for the blessing of our food on this day. We ask for continued healing for those afflicted in spirit, mind, or body. We ask for protection for those that are suffering through domestic violence and abuse. For those that have lost loved ones, we ask for comfort to be granted. We ask for an ease of tensions and divisions that separate us from our brothers and sisters. We ask for protection for our animal brothers the wolf, bear, horse, buffalo, whale, and dolphin. We ask for greater understanding that all life is precious and sacred. We ask for an end to environmental abuse and destruction. We ask for greater awareness and compassion toward the homeless and the poor. We ask for open doors to those that are seeking work. We ask for an end to the materialistic desires that control us. We ask for a time of true equality where no one is more powerful than the next. We ask for an era of peace and tranquility where all four colors can unite for the common good. We ask for a greater spiritual awakening during this time of purification, so we may begin the arduous task for restoring balance to ourselves, Mother Earth, and strengthening the spirit that dwells in all your children.

We thank you for the early morning mist as it floats down from above. We thank you for the morning breeze that caresses our cheeks and brings a sense of peace to our spirit. We thank you for the wisdom that can be found in nature that will find its way into our hearts. We thank you for the rainforests that provide us with the air to breathe. We thank you for the guidance you provide as we begin a new day. So, it is. So shall it be.

reat Spirit, Almighty Healer, and Creator of all things, it is with humble hearts that we unite to send up many thanks. We thank you for the many trials throughout our lifetime that strengthen us. We thank you for the many relationships we have had that give us wisdom later on in life. We thank you for the trees that give us air to breathe and shelter when we are in need. We thank you for the many herbs and plants that we use to cure ailments and diseases. We thank you for the water that hydrates our bodies.

We ask for continued healing for those that are suffering through afflictions of the spirit, body, or mind. We ask for protection and freedom for those of our children that have been taken from their homes. We ask for your comfort and peace for those that may have lost loved ones. We ask for a new era of peace and wars to not enter our minds again. We ask for more hardened hearts to soften and closed eyes to see what we must do to repair the damage we have done to our Earth Mother. We ask for an end to the hatred, deception, racism, greed, and lust for power that can be found across the four corners. We ask for guidance each day as we journey along our paths. We ask for strength when we are weak; understanding when we are fearful; and peace when we are agitated. We ask for a great unity be granted throughout the four corners and four colors. May the era of purification and awakening be as strong as unwavering winds.

We thank you for your mercy and forgiveness. We thank you for our daily food and ask for its blessing. We thank you for our elders that bring us wisdom and life lessons, in a world where so few can understand and walk the path of their ancestors. May we honor them with respect. We thank you for our children that remind us of lessons long forgotten and the next generation to build upon the foundation we have set before them. We thank you for our relations, families and friends that help to strengthen us when we tend to be weary. For the greatest gift of life, we thank you. So, it is. So shall it be.

G reat Spirit, Almighty Healer, and Creator of all things, we unite this day with humble hearts to give many thanks. We thank you for all the gifts and blessings that you have given us. Many times, we just accept them without realizing that they are for a purpose and come with great responsibility. We thank you for our lives and the lives of our children. We thank you for the unique paths you have set before us. May we learn early in life those paths and may we walk them with strength and conviction. We thank you for our ancestors that still remain with us in spirit, and their wisdom and guidance.

We ask for better understanding and guidance during this time of change. May we leave our selfishness behind us and replace it with the understanding that we were not given this opportunity to waste on ourselves. We ask for deliverance from the bad wolves in our governments that are only looking to control, obtain more power, and become wealthier. We ask that they begin to feed the good wolf more and do what their people elected them to do. We ask for healing in both body and soul for those that are in great need. We ask for the end of hatred, bigotry, racism, and greed during this time of change. We ask for the release of Leonard Peltier and others that have been wrongfully imprisoned. We ask for protection for our animal friends that face dangers from those who would hunt them down for sport.

We thank you for Mother Earth and her many treasures of cures, wisdom, food, and so much more. We thank you for the music and the wisdom you send in the gentle winds that come. We thank you for our elders that give us all we need to continue down our paths. May we pass their lessons, love, and wisdom onto the next generation to build upon and bring them the respect they deserve. We thank you for this time of change. May we give up the ways we have been taught over the past few generations and begin to do what we were given our paths to do. We thank you for your love and forgiveness and the guidance you provide us each day. So, it is. So shall it be.

reat Spirit, Almighty Healer, and Creator of all things, it is with humble hearts that we gather together to send up many thanks. For the flowing of waters from the mountaintops that come to hydrate our bodies, we thank you. We thank you for the many herbs that you provide to cure our diseases and ailments. May we learn to use them instead of the man-made poisons called pharmaceuticals. We thank you for our food and water and ask for their blessing.

We ask for your protection as we stand against those that are destroying your creation and placing our Earth Mother out of balance. May we unite to regain balance as it was long ago. We ask for guidance for all that you have given the power to reverse the process of many years to bring about change. We ask for healing for those that are suffering from afflictions of spirit, mind, and body. We ask for an end to the wars that only allow for suffering of many people. We ask instead for peace to bring about the necessary change throughout many countries and allow our children to return home. We ask for an end to hatred, greed, racism, and lust of materialism. May we all become equal once again and learn to be proper caretakers of the land.

We thank you for our elders and the wisdom and lessons they give us. May we continue to honor them as we should. We thank you for our children that will continue to bring about change from the foundation we have set for them. We thank you for our animal friends that bring joy and comfort to us and ask for their protection from those that would willfully destroy them without cause. We thank you most of all for the gift of life that allows us to do this. So, it is. So shall it be.

Great Spirit, Almighty Healer, and Creator of all things, it is with humble hearts that we come together, as one, to offer up many thanks. We thank you for the babbling brooks that cascade down from the mountain peaks. We thank you for the serenity we find by the waterfall, as it reaches down into the lagoon. We thank you for the vegetation and trees that are found in the forest. We thank you for the coolness of the early morning air. We thank you for the beauty of the wild berries of the woodlands. For the songs of the fliers, as we awaken during the rising of the sun's golden hue.

We ask for the release of the downtrodden, that have been subjected to horrendous life from their leaders. We ask that you also protect our leadership and their families. We ask for the strength and courage to do the tasks you have given us. We ask for a return to the days where we focused our lives around you, through faith and prayer. We ask for miraculous healing for those that are suffering through afflictions of the spirit, mind, or body. For those that are grieving the loss of loved ones, we ask for strength, comfort and peace to be granted them. We ask for an era of peace, far from the violence of those that refuse to see the value of life.

We thank you for our elders that give us the wisdom of the past, as well as the lessons of the present. We thank you for our children that continue to show us the innocence we've lost through the years. We thank you for our family and friends, that continue to support and strengthen us during our time in need. We thank you for your love, forgiveness, direction, and courage each day. We thank you for answering our prayers. We thank you for our food and ask for its blessing. So, it is. So shall it be.

reat Spirit, Almighty Healer, and Creator of all things, with humble hearts we unite to send up many thanks. We thank you for the soft flowing winds that bring the music to soothe our spirits. We thank you for the flowing waters as it rushes from the mountaintops to hydrate our bodies. For the food we receive each day, we thank you and ask for its blessing. We thank you for the trees that bring us wisdom and the air to breathe. We thank you for the herbs that you have given to cure our ailments and diseases. May we learn to use them as we should.

We ask for the healing of our relations that are suffering through afflictions of the spirit, mind, or body. We ask for more hearts to soften and to bring understanding to those that have found themselves ignorant of the plight of the First Nation people. We ask for an end to selfish desire of materialistic items. We ask for an end to the lust for power and money, so we may once again become equal. No man higher than the other. We ask for protection and guidance for those that are standing against governments in order to have treaties honored. We ask for protection of all of our animal friends that are facing great danger from those who wish to bring home trophies for their walls. We ask for an end to hatred, greed, racism, and discrimination.

We thank you for our elders as they bring us wisdom and necessary lessons to guide us during our journey. May we continue to honor them as we should. We thank you for our children that bring us innocence and lessons long forgotten. May we erect an unbreakable foundation for them to build upon. We thank you for the gift of life and your forgiveness when we tend to stray from our path. So, it is. So shall it be.

reat Spirit, Almighty Healer, and Creator of all things, we gather with humbled hearts and minds to offer up many thanks. We thank you for the early morning dawn as the sun rises to light our paths and provide warmth. We thank you for the winter as it prepares to rejuvenate the lands and bring us new herbs and plants. We thank you for the trees that give us the air to breathe. We thank you for the waters that rush down from the mountaintops to hydrate us each day.

We ask for continued healing for those that are suffering from afflictions of the spirit, mind, or body. We ask for an end to dangerous pharmaceuticals and more people discover that all cures can be found in the plants and herbs that you have provided. We ask for guidance for those that stand against continued oppression. We ask for protection for our animal friends, the horse, bear, wolf, buffalo, whale, dolphin, and all that may be facing death and extermination. We ask for freedom for those that have been falsely imprisoned and find themselves political prisoners of evil regimes. We ask for an end to the hatred, greed, racism, and materialistic lust that can be found throughout the four corners. For those that find themselves in modern day slavery, we ask for their freedom as well, Father.

We thank you for our elders that provide us with the necessary wisdom and life lessons as we travel our paths each day. May we continue to honor them as we should. We thank you for our children that remind us of lessons long forgotten. We thank you for our daily food and ask for its blessing. We thank you for the gift of life and the opportunity to regain balance to our Earth Mother. We thank you for the mysteries of the universe that surrounds us. So, it is. So shall it be.

Great Spirit, Almighty Healer, and Creator of all things, it is with humble hearts that we unite to offer up many thanks. We thank you for the wide expanse and mysterious universe that surrounds us. We thank you for the many blessings and gifts that you have given. May we learn to use them for the betterment of all. We thank you for the rising of the sun each morning to light our paths and provide warmth. We thank you for its setting in the evening with its colors of red, orange, and purple.

We ask for your comfort and peace to be given to those that have lost loved ones. We ask for guidance and strength for those that have passed over into the Spirit World. We ask for great healing for those that are suffering both physically and spiritually and give them the peace they desire. We ask for hardened hearts to break loose of the chains that bind them. We ask for those that are missing to find their way home. For those that may be fighting overseas and under the earth, we ask for their safe return to their loved ones. We ask for an end to the wrongful taking of children from their families. We ask for guidance and protection to be given to those that stand against those the further destruction of your creation. We ask for protection for all two-legged, four-legged, swimmers, fliers and crawlers that are facing grave danger. May we all learn and understand the sacredness of all life and stop hunting for the sake of trophies.

We thank you for the moon as it watches over us during our slumber. We thank you for Father Sky as he continues to protect us from the hazards of space. For Mother Earth that provides us with the cures, hydration, and air to breathe, we thank you. We thank you for the wisdom and knowledge that is imparted upon us. We thank you for the knowledge of our true selves and the vibrating energy that will allow us to ascend to the next level of existence. So, it is. So shall it be.

reat Spirit, Almighty Healer, and Creator of all things, we gather with humble hearts to send up many thanks. We thank you for the gift of life and the unique paths you have set before us. We thank you for the many gifts that you have bestowed upon us. May we learn to use them for the betterment of all. We thank you for the two-legged, four-legged, swimmers, crawlers and fliers that inhabit the earth. May we learn to understand and respect them as we should. We thank you for our elders that continue to teach wisdom of the old ways and life lessons in the present. May we honor them with deep respect as we should. We thank you for our children that will inherit the land. May we instruct them on the importance of their land and how to properly care for it.

We ask for continued healing for those that are still suffering from afflictions of the spirit, mind, or body. We ask for an end to our selfishness and greed so we may begin refocusing to rid ourselves of polluted air and water. We ask for strength, guidance and courage to help heal our Earth Mother. We ask for protection for our animal friends that are facing death through the hands of the wicked for sport. We ask for an end to modern-day slavery and the return of the lost ones back home. We ask for an end to war, and a beginning of peace. We ask for an end to hatred, bigotry, racism, lust of money, and power. We ask for a strong awakening where more spirits begin to understand the damage done and guidance to help in the repair of your creation.

We thank you for the great expanse of the universe that surrounds us. We thank you for the prayers that have been answered and those that will come in time. We thank you for the trees and rain forests that provide the air we breathe. We thank you for the flowing waters from snow-capped mountains to the seas below. We thank you for reminding us each morning just how precious life really is. So, it is. So shall it be.

Great Spirit, Almighty Healer, and Creator of all things, we unite with humbled hearts to offer up many thanks. We thank you for the blessings and gifts that you have bestowed upon us. We thank you for answered and unanswered prayers. We thank you for your forgiveness when we stray. We thank you for our elders that give us the guidance and wisdom that has been passed throughout the generations. May we honor them with deep respect as we should. We thank you for our children that provide us with both innocence and lessons long forgotten.

We ask for a growing spiritual awakening as the momentum from the movement continues to grow. We ask for guidance for those that desire to change the fate of our Earth Mother into restoring her beauty. We ask for strength and comfort for those that are suffering both spiritually and physically, Father. We ask for an age of peace to replace this age of hatred and misunderstanding. For those that have spent so much time away from nature, we ask for their hardened hearts to be softened. We ask for an end to the materialistic lust that controls our lives and hope for a growing spiritual revival. We ask for protection for our animal friends that face grave danger. We ask for freedom for those that have been imprisoned without cause, and for those that have found themselves in modern-day slavery.

We thank you for the great expanse of the universe and all the wonders yet to be discovered. We thank you for the sacred circles found in all your creation. We thank you for our Earth Mother as she provides us with life sustaining plants, herbs, and waters. So, it is. So shall it be.

Great Spirit, Almighty Healer, and Creator of all things, we unite with humbled hearts to offer up many thanks. We thank you for the gift of life, you have breathed into every living thing. We thank you for the many blessings and gifts you have given us. We thank you for all two-legged, four-legged, swimmers, fliers, and crawlers that we may interact with each day. We thank you for each new golden sunrise that reminds us of the gift of each new day granted. We thank you for the beauty of the sunset, with its hues of red, orange, and yellow.

We have allowed materialistic greed and money to control us. We ask for your forgiveness and guidance toward returning to a time, where we were better caretakers of your creation. We have polluted the lands, waters and sky and have brought hatred, corruption, and division where we were once united in peace. We ask for a return to an era of this peace, and use the gifts provided, to bring back balance to a world that is bent on destroying itself. We ask for protection for our animal brothers and sisters that are facing grave danger from men, that have lost all understanding and love of life. We ask for protection for the women and children that continue to suffer through violence and abuse. We ask for strength, guidance, and courage, as we stand against those that would continue to destroy the lands, waters, and skies above. We ask for an end to the corruption, greed and lust of power and wealth of those that are supposed to serve their people. We ask for an end to the division that continues to keep your people from uniting. We ask for hardened hearts to soften and compassion be used to help the poor, homeless, widows and all that are in need. We ask for a greater spiritual awakening in hearts that have been bound by stereotype and racist views for too long. We ask for the return of our children that have been missing from their families. We ask for eyes of the lost to open enough to see all that has been hidden and the evil intentions that have been placed upon them.

We thank you for our many trials as they bring strength to our spirits. We thank you for our elders as they bring us the instruction and wisdom needed to follow our path. We thank you for our children that will build upon the foundation we have set before them. We thank you for our relations that interact with us each day to give us insight in areas of misunderstanding. We thank you for our family and friends that give us the support we need along our journey. We thank you for the knowledge and wisdom that you have given. We thank you for the prophecies, found in the scriptures, that we are see being fulfilled in our lifetime. So, it is. So shall it be.

Great Spirit, Almighty Healer, and Creator of all things, with humble hearts we gather together to offer many thanks. We thank you for the precious gift of life and the unique paths provided to us. May we strive to follow them with strong legs and straight eyes. We thank you for our elders that bring us insight and wisdom to help us along our journey. May we hold them with the deepest respect they deserve. We thank you for our children that will carry these onto the next generation and build upon the unbreakable foundation the seventh generation is erecting now. We thank you for our family and friends that give us the support we need. We thank you for our animal friends and the Holy Spirit that bring comfort to us in our time of need.

We ask for your healing hands to be placed upon those that are suffering from diverse diseases and disorders. We ask for comfort for those that have lost loved ones. We ask for guidance, strength, and courage for those that are meeting their ancestors in the Spirit World for their next phase of life. We ask for guidance as we continue along our paths and bring discernment when it is in need. We ask for great visions and dreams for your children during this time, and blessing our hearts so we may hear and understand them. We ask for an era of peace in a world where your children are exhausted over the hatred, greed, and lust for power behind the wars we must endure. We ask for the veils of secrecy to be lifted so your children can better understand how and why governmental policies are forced upon us. We ask for an end to the hatred and stereotypes that divide your people. We ask for protection for our animal brothers and sisters that are facing grave dangers each day. We ask for protection for our women and children that continue to endure violence and abuse. We ask for protection and freedom for those that have been taken from their homes. As in war, we too are tired of our children being abducted and killed to satisfy the greed and lust of the abductors. For as we have trespassed against others, we also ask for forgiveness for those of our enemies. We ask for doors to open, and compassion given to our homeless, widows, children and those struggling in poverty.

We thank you for the rain that comes to bring moisture and growth to the plants and herbs. We thank you for the wisdom of the heart. We thank you for the music found in the rushing waters and gentle winds in nature. We thank you for the understanding that the answers we seek can all be found in nature if we take the time to empty our minds and truly listen to our surroundings. We thank you for the rain forests that give us the air to breathe. So, it is. So shall it be.

Great Spirit, Almighty Healer, and Creator of all things, it is with humble hearts that we unite together to offer up many thanks. We thank you for the spirit that dwells within our hearts and the hearts of all living things. We thank you for our ancestors that are still with us in spirit and the wisdom they bring to us. We thank you for all the two-legged, four-legged, swimmers, fliers and crawlers that are with us. We thank you for the music found in the gentle winds that flow through the trees and the flowing waters. We thank you for the trials we endure to strengthen us and prepare us for what lies ahead. We thank you for the many answered prayers. We thank you for the gracefulness of the ocean waves as they gently caress the sandy shore. For the swaying of the palm and willow during the afternoon wind, we thank you. We thank you for the golden colors of the morning sunrise to the reddish hues of the evening setting.

We ask for your healing hands to be placed upon those that are suffering from man-made and natural diseases and disorders. We ask for a greater awakening during this time, so we may begin the long struggle of bringing back balance. We ask for an end to the turmoil that has kept your people divided for too long, so we may bring back balance. We ask for an end to such hatred, greed, lust of power and materialism that is found in our governments and corporations, that have filled the hearts of those that have become complacent and naive. We ask for freedom for those that have been abducted or taken from their homes without cause. We ask for protection for your forests, waters, plains, and deserts that man has taken parts of your creation without replacing. We ask for strength, guidance, and courage for those that stand against governments that do not protect the lands, or the treaties they have signed. We ask for freedom for those, like our Brother Leonard Peltier, that have been imprisoned without just cause. We ask for protection for all two-legged, four-legged, swimmers, fliers and crawlers that are facing grave danger. May we be of strong heart and defend all that are defenseless. We ask for guidance each day, so we may travel our paths with courage, strong legs, and straight eyes. We ask for more compassion to be placed upon the hearts of those that are aware of the homelessness in their cities. We ask for more open doors for them, so they may once again be able to live productive lives.

We thank you for our elders that show us many life lessons and wisdom to carry within us during our journey. May we always endeavor to bring great honor to them. We thank you for our children that continue to teach us innocence and lessons long forgotten. May we provide them with an unbreakable foundation from which they will build on. We thank you for our relations that interact with us during the day that strengthen our spirits. We thank you for the gift of life and the paths you have given us. We thank you for the wisdom of the heart. May we learn to listen intently before we speak and understand that there is strength in silence. So, it is. So shall it be.

Great Spirit, Almighty Healer, and Creator of all things, it is with a humble heart that we come together as one to offer up many thanks. We thank you for the knowledge that all things were created with a purpose. We thank you for the lifeblood for all living things and providing us with the necessities of life, from the water we drink, our daily food, and the shelter that keeps us safe. We thank you for all that is found in nature, from the many herbs and plants to nourish and provide cures, to the multitudes of four legged, fliers, crawlers and swimmers. We thank you for the cycle of life found throughout all the things you have created.

We ask for peace in a world that has been dominated with violence through the misunderstanding and stereotyping of religion, cultures, and ethnicity. We ask for mindsets that have been brainwashed toward the deception placed upon them for decades, to be changed to that of love, compassion and understanding of all peoples. May we work toward helping those in need, rather than believing in the adage of "survival of the fittest" mentality. We ask for miraculous healing for those that are suffering through the various diseases and disorders. We ask for former and future treaties with any country or indigenous tribe be honored with integrity, and may the conditions always be adhered to. In the past, this country has never honored their treaties with the Native Americans, we pray that they now will honor the promises in this generation. May our word now be our bond once again. We continue to ask for an end to the greed, discrimination, and materialism that divides us. We ask for a time where we can be united to repair the damage we have done over the centuries.

We thank you for the knowledge that you have all things under your control. Though we may not completely understand why some things happen, may we learn to surrender all things to you and have the faith to know that, like all things, there is a purpose. We thank you for our children that continue to inspire, and for the elders that continue to teach. We thank you for the sacredness of all life. We thank you for our daily food and ask for its blessing. So, it is. So shall it be.

Great Spirit, Almighty Healer, and Creator of all things, with humble hearts we gather to offer many thanks. We thank you for the sacredness of the circle; the four seasons, the life cycle, and all things found throughout the majestic Universe that surrounds us. We thank you for the cool flowing waters that race down from the snowcapped mountains. We thank you for our daily food and ask for its blessing. We thank you for the rainforests that supply us with the air we need. We thank you for the precious gift of life and all the wonderment our eyes behold. We thank you for the rainbow, that reminds us of your covenant with us, that this planet will not be destroyed by flood again.

We are weary, Father. We tend to wander aimlessly around the turmoil that surrounds us when we should be more focused upon you. We ask for your guidance, peace, and strength as we continue to walk our unique paths. We are weary of the hatred, greed, lust of wealth and power. We ask for your strength and eyes, like the hawk, that remain steadfast on the task at hand. We ask for the strength of the eagle as it flies above the storm clouds. We are weary of seeing the abuse and violence our women and children are subjected to. We ask for courage to stand for the defenseless. Many have lost their way and we ask that their spirits be reawakened. We ask for comfort and guidance for those that are low in spirit. We are weary of the carnage by the hands of those that hunt for sport and trophies. We ask for courage and strength to stand against those that would further harm the animals, the wolf, bear, buffalo, horse, whale, and dolphin. We ask for a world promised where we can finally live in peace. We ask for greater compassion toward those that are in great need. May we return to the days of our ancestors where we helped those that struggle to survive. We ask for your healing hands to be placed upon those that are suffering through afflictions of the spirit, mind, or body. For those that have lost loved ones, we ask for your comfort and peace to be granted them. We ask that you open our hearts, minds, and ears to listen and discern, as your instruction is given to us.

We thank you for our ancestors that remain with us and bring us wisdom. We thank you for our family and friends that interact with us each day and supply us with the support we need. We thank you for all two-legged, four-legged, swimmers, fliers, and crawlers. We thank you for the sight of the robin as it pecks the soil for its food. So, it is. So shall it be.

Great Spirit, Almighty Healer, and Creator of all things, it is with humble hearts that we congregate to offer up requests alongside our deepest gratitude. We thank you for the season of renewal where new life is formed. We thank you for the season of growth where planted seeds have reached their optimum growth. We thank you for the season of harvest with its woodland covering of diverse colored leaves. We thank you for the season of slumber that Mother Earth uses to rest and prepare for the next cycle.

We ask for a return of the ancient days while life was innocent and according to your purpose. We ask for an end to the dark forces that have enslaved your children for too long. We ask for truth to find its way once again into the minds of those of us that remain during this transition. We ask for an end to fear that has kept us down. We ask for a new beginning where we are guided on the right path. We ask that the proud become humbled; the hateful become more loving; the hoarders become more giving. We ask for an end to the unlawful taxation that has served to keep us too busy to ask questions. We ask for what is rightfully ours and to return us to a place of prominence and prosperity. We ask for an end to the lawlessness. We ask for a righting of the ship where things become as they were in the beginning before Adam and Eve listened to the serpent. We ask for an end to homelessness. For those that need healing of their afflictions of the mind, body, or spirit, we ask for that to be granted.

We thank you for the guidance you send so we may follow our path with strong legs and straight eyes. We thank you for our elders that have given us tools we need along our journey. We thank you for our children that will carry the lessons and wisdom on to the next generation. We thank you for our thorns that keep us from becoming too proud or boastful. We thank you for the music that accompanies the coolness of the evening air. So, it is. So shall it be.

Great Spirit, Almighty Healer, and Creator of all things, with humbled hearts we gather to offer many thanks. We thank you for the sacredness of the circle; the four seasons, the life cycle, and all things found throughout the majestic Universe that surrounds us. We thank you for the cool flowing waters that race down from the snowcapped mountains. We thank you for our daily food and ask for its blessing. We thank you for the rainforests that supply us with the air we need. We thank you for the sun, the moon, sky, and our earth. We thank you for the precious gift of life and all the wonderment our eyes behold. We thank you for the rainbow, that reminds us of your covenant with us, that this planet will not be destroyed by flood again. We thank you for the sight of the robin as it pecks the soil for its food.

We are weary, Father. We tend to wander aimlessly around the turmoil that surrounds us when we should be more focused upon you. We ask for your guidance, peace, and strength as we continue to walk our unique paths. We are weary of the hatred, greed, lust of wealth and power. We ask for your strength and eyes, like the hawk, that remain steadfast on the task at hand. We ask for the strength of the eagle as it flies above the storm clouds. We are weary of seeing the abuse and violence our women and children are subjected to. We ask for courage to stand for the defenseless. We are weary of the tarnishment of litter that invades the waters and lands. We ask for your forgiveness, and the softening of hearts that have been hardened for so long. Many have lost their way and we ask that their spirits be reawakened. We ask for comfort and guidance for those that are low in spirit. We are weary of the carnage by the hands of those that hunt for sport and trophies. We ask for courage and strength to stand against those that would further harm the animals, the wolf, bear, buffalo, horse, whale, and dolphin. We ask for a world promised where we can finally live in peace. We ask for greater compassion toward those that are in great need. May we return to the days of our ancestors where we helped those that struggle to survive. We ask for your healing hands to be placed upon those that are suffering through diverse diseases, disorders, and ailments. For those that have lost loved ones, we ask for your comfort and peace be granted to them. We ask that you open our hearts, minds, and ears to listen and discern, as your instruction is given to us.

We thank you for our elders that give us the lessons and wisdom we need as we continue to follow the path of honor. We thank you for our children that will take these lessons and pass them on to future generations. We thank you for our ancestors that remain with us and bring us wisdom. We thank you for our family and friends that interact with us each day and supply us with the support we need. We thank you for all two-legged, four-legged, swimmers, fliers, and crawlers. So, it is. So shall it be.

Great Spirit, Almighty Healer, and Creator of all things, it is with humble hearts that we unify at the rising of the sun, to send up requests alongside our deepest gratitude. We thank you for the gentle winds as we arise to greet the day. We thank you for the beauty of watching the fliers that do their morning circle dance in the air. We thank you for the music that flows from the early morning winds, the fliers, and the crawlers. We thank you for the reminder that life is but a gift to your children and that each of us has a purpose.

We ask for guidance on this day as we walk our paths. May we walk with strength and conviction. We begin to hear the heartbeat of Mother Earth as the day of change draws near, we ask for more hearts to be awakened. We ask for an end to the division, hatred and greed that darkens our souls throughout all nations. We ask instead for peace and love to move forward. We ask for the hearts and minds of the governments to break free of the power of greed, so they may do what they were elected to do. We ask for healing for all your children that are suffering greatly, Father. May your healing hands be placed upon them and give them wholeness, strength, and comfort. We ask for your guidance, love and peace to be given to those children that are away from their homes for various reasons, to be returned safely.

We thank you for the many blessings you have bestowed upon us. We thank you for your forgiveness when we stray from our path. May we always walk in prayer. We thank you for the majestic mountains to the seas below and all life that find peace in you. We thank you for the wide expanse of the universe that surrounds us. We thank you for our elders, children, and all relations that teach us many things. So, it is. So shall it be.

Great Spirit, Almighty Healer, and Creator of all things throughout this universe, we unite this day with humble hearts to send up requests alongside our deepest thankfulness. We thank you for the rising of the sun that allows us to arise and greet the new day. We thank you for the blessing of life and the paths you have set before us. We thank you for the forests, oceans, and deserts that are all teaming with life. We thank you for solitude when we can go out each day to reflect on the spirit and behold the life that surrounds us. We thank you for the spirit that connects all living things. We thank you for your patience, love, and guidance.

We ask for continued healing for those that are suffering through the afflictions of mind, body, or spirit. We ask for strength, comfort, and guidance for loved ones that have moved on into the Spirit World. We ask for guidance each day as we travel down our unique paths. We ask for an end to the hatred that grows within the hearts of those that do not or will not look for understanding. We ask for protection for those that have been taken from their homes and led into slavery. We ask for strength, comfort, and freedom for those that have been wrongfully imprisoned. We ask for an end to materialism that feeds the greed among us. We ask for more souls to join us in the upcoming change and begin to unite the world. We ask for peace and an end to wars.

We thank you for the gentle winds that bring us the music that soothes our souls. We thank you for the trees that provide us with the air we breathe. We thank you for the waters that flow from the mountaintops to the seas below that hydrate our bodies. We thank you for the good soil that allows for plants and herbs to grow. We thank you for our daily food and ask for its blessing. We thank you for your creation that surrounds us all. May we begin to undo the damage we have done over the centuries. We thank you for the universe that surrounds us. May we remind ourselves that all of creation is connected as one. So, it is. So shall it be.

Great Spirit, Almighty Healer, and Creator of all things, with humble hearts we gather together to offer up many thanks. We thank you for the sacredness of the circle; the four seasons, the life cycle, and all things found throughout the majestic universe that surrounds us. We thank you for the cold cascading waters that race down from the snowcapped mountains. We thank you for the rainforests that supply us with the air we need. We thank you for the sun, moon, sky, and our Mother Earth. We thank you for the precious gift of life and all the awe-inspiring wonders our eyes behold. We thank you for the tranquility and wisdom found in nature. We thank you for the clouds above that bring the rain and snow to areas of need. We thank you for the cool autumn nights, surrounded by family and friends, around the campfire. We thank you for the call of the wolf and coyote in the evening hours.

We are weary, Father. We tend to wander aimlessly around the turmoil that surrounds us. We ask for your guidance, peace, and strength as we continue to walk our unique paths. We are weary of violence and carnage, and ask for an era of peace and unity. We are weary of leaders that say one thing and do another. We ask for judgment against those that run contrary to the spirit connected to all things. We are weary of the hatred, greed, lust for wealth and power. We ask for eyes, like the hawk, that remain steadfast on the task at hand. We ask for the strength of the eagle as it flies above the storm clouds. We are weary of seeing the abuse and violence our women and children are subjected to. We ask for courage to stand for the defenseless. We are weary of the litter that invades the waters and lands. We ask for your forgiveness and the softening of hearts that have been hardened for so long. Many have lost their way and we ask that their spirits be reawakened and break the chains that have bound them. We ask for comfort and guidance for those that are low in spirit. We are weary of the carnage of the hands of those that hunt for sport and trophies. We ask for a world promised where we can finally live in peace. We ask for greater compassion toward those that are in great need. May we return to the days of our ancestors where we helped those that struggled to survive. We ask for your healing hands to be placed upon those that are suffering through diverse diseases, pestilences, disorders, and ailments. For those that have lost loved ones, we ask for your comfort and peace to be given. We ask for judgement upon those that have deceived the masses while perpetrating their evil upon the world.

We thank you for our elders that give us the lessons and wisdom we need. We thank you for our children that will take these lessons and pass them on to future generations. We thank you for our family and friends that interact with us each day and supply us with the support we need. We thank you for all two-legged, four-legged, swimmers, fliers, and crawlers. We thank you for your love and mercy when we obey your word; your discipline when we stray. We thank you for our daily food and ask for its blessing. So, it is. So shall it be.

Great Spirit, Almighty Healer, and Creator of all things, it is with a humble heart that we unite to send up requests alongside our deepest gratitude. We thank you for the mysteries in the universe that surrounds us. We thank you for the wisdom and the strong spirit found in our hearts that connects us to all things. We thank you for the many visions and dreams you have sent to us. We thank you for our ancestors that continue to supply us with the wisdom of the old ways. We thank you for each new day and the precious gift of life.

We ask for forgiveness when we have not listened to or obeyed your words. We ask for guidance, strength, and courage to move forward and defend the defenseless and begin to repair the damage we have done. We have exploited your creation simply for our own ends, distorted our knowledge and abused our power. We ask for guidance and patience to clean the air we breathe, the water we drink, and the land we inhabit. We ask for strength, guidance, and courage to stand against those that have taken at will and have not replenished. We ask for continued healing for those that are suffering through afflictions of the mind, body, or spirit. We ask for hardened hearts to soften, clogged ears to open, and closed eyes to see what we must do to repair the damage we have done to our planet. We ask for an end to the hatred, racism, greed and lust of power and materialism that can be found across the four corners. We ask for protection for our women and children enduring violence and abuse. We ask for an end to the violence and control that seeks to divide us.

We thank you for the trees that give us air to breathe; the many herbs and plants to cure ailments and diseases; and the waters that flow from the mountaintops to hydrate our bodies. We thank you for the many trials that strengthen our spirits. We thank you for our relations found across the great waters that join us as prophesies of the ancients begin to unfold. We thank you for introducing new family and friends into our lives. May your blessings be upon them. So, it is. So shall it be.

Great Spirit, Almighty Healer, and Creator of all things, it is with a humbled heart that we gather to offer many thanks. We send this prayer to thank you, Father, for the many things that have been bestowed upon us. We thank you for the rising of the sun each morning as she brings light, warmth, and photosynthesis for growth. We thank you for every waking hour reminding us of the gift of life. We thank you for the dew and mists, that moistens the soil, the many plants, and diverse herbs. We thank you for the wrens and finches that awaken us with the soft music they provide. We thank you for the rain as it provides growth and purification. We thank you for the lightning storms that create nitrates in the soil allowing for further growth of plant life. We thank you for the knowledge we obtain when we observe nature away from urban life.

We thank you for the gentle winds that give us wisdom and music when we learn to listen. We thank you for the rushing of the waters flowing from the mountaintops to the lakes and oceans below, teaming with swimmers, and hydrating our bodies. We thank you for the rain forests that give us the air to breathe. We thank you for all the two-legged, four-legged, swimmers, fliers and crawlers that surround us each day. We thank you for the grassy plains, thick forests and jungles, desolate deserts, and the glaciers of the north. We thank you for our daily food and ask for its blessing. We thank you for the four seasons that mirror the cycle of life. We thank you for the eagle and his reminder that we should live our lives soaring above the many storms. We thank you for our family and friends, that help to guide us along our path. We thank you for the opening of the veil that allows us to see that which has been hidden.

We thank you for the sky as it protects us day and night from the hazards of space. We thank you for Mother Earth as she nourishes, heals, and hydrates us. We thank you for our elders that give us the wisdom and instruction we need along our journey. We thank you for our children that will soon begin building upon the foundation set by the generation before them. We thank you for our ancestors and the wisdom and instruction that they continue to provide, through the stories that are told. We thank you for your forgiveness when we stray. We thank you for your love, guidance and strength that enable us to move forward along our path. We thank you for the Spirit World and the knowledge that life does not end here. So, it is. So shall it be.

Great Spirit, Almighty Healer, and Creator of all things, we united with humbled hearts to offer up requests alongside our many thanks. We thank you for the rising of Grandfather Sun as he continues to provide the necessary photosynthesis to plant life. We thank you for the moon as it watches over us during our slumber. We thank you for the sky that protects us from the radiation from space each day. We thank you for Mother Earth as she supplies us with all that we need to survive. We thank you for the gift of life that you have breathed into every living thing. We thank you for the sounds of the frogs, crickets, and grasshoppers; music of the wren and finch; and the howls of the wolf and coyote. We thank you for the soaring of the hawk and the eagle overhead. We thank you for the swaying of the grasslands of the plains, as the afternoon breeze flows through each blade of grain. We thank you for the majestic mountains, as they tower over the valleys. We thank you for the soft sands upon the shore, and the gracefulness of the waves of the ocean waters.

We have allowed materialistic greed and money to control us. We ask for your forgiveness and guidance toward returning to a time where we were better caretakers of your creation, where we understood to be more selfless than selfish. We have polluted the lands, waters, and sky, and have brought hatred, corruption, and division. We ask for a return to an era of peace, where we use the gifts provided to bring back balance to a world that is destroying itself. We ask for protection for our animal brothers and sisters, facing grave danger from men that lost all understanding and love of life. We ask for protection for the women and children that continue to suffer through violence and abuse. We ask for an end to the division that continues to keep your people from uniting and fulfilling the prophecies. We ask for hardened hearts to soften and compassion be used to help the poor, homeless, widows, and all that are in need. We ask for comfort, strength, and guidance toward those that are low in spirit and suffering through betrayal or self-worth. We ask for your guidance in providing empowerment to those that are in need.

We thank you for our many trials as they bring strength to our spirits. We thank you for our elders as they bring us the instruction and wisdom needed to follow our path. We thank you for our children that will build upon the foundation we have set before them. We thank you for our relations that interact with us each day to give us insight into areas of misunderstanding. We thank you for our family and friends that give us the support we need along our journey. We thank you for the many blessings and gifts you have given us. So, it is. So shall it be.

Great Spirit, Almighty Healer, and Creator of all things both seen and unseen, it is with a humble heart that we offer many thanks. We thank you for the denseness of the forests that allow the four-legged to flourish among the trees, plants and herbs. We thank you for the desolate deserts that give life to the crawlers amid the cacti, aloe, and Joshua trees. We thank you for the rainforest that gives life to the fliers and four-legged amid the indigenous people and the many herbs that bring us the cures for our ailments.

We ask for your mercy and forgiveness for our misdeeds and arrogance. We have thought too highly of ourselves when we should have thought more of others. We have squandered our lives for riches and fame when we should have been feeding the hungry and giving them shelter and clothing. We have taken from the Earth without replacing and not allowing time for her regeneration. We ask for a time where understanding and love enter the hearts of all people, to bring back the balance. We ask for peace and tranquility, where there is violence and hatred. We ask for patience when we try to do things ourselves instead of handing them to you. We ask for unity where there is division so that we can do the tasks that you originally gave us. We ask for an end to our addictions that prevent us from following your will and guidance. We ask for greater morality to enter the hearts of those that lead.

We thank you for our friends, both near and far, that continue to provide us with the insight that we need. We thank you for our family that give us support during times of indecision. We thank you for those of our elders that give us lessons and wisdom from the past to the present. We thank you for our children that continue to remind us of what we have forgotten, as well as new insight they have learned. We thank you for our food and ask for its blessing. For the lifeblood for our hydration and the air for our bodies, we thank you. So, it is. So shall it be.

Great Spirit, Almighty Healer, and Creator of all things, it is with a humble heart that we assemble to offer many thanks. We thank you for the beauty of the salmon as it continues to defy the odds, and swims upstream to spawn. We thank you for the water cascading down from the mountainside, that give us the necessary hydration for our bodies. We thank you for the knowledge that we are created from the earth, and therefore a part of her. We thank you for the worms and ants that aerate the soil, allowing for new growth. We thank you for stillness of the lakes and oceans in the early morning hours, as the sun slowly begins to spread its golden hue. We thank you for the aroma of the salty sea air, and the briskness of the air coming off the ocean waters. We thank you for the swaying of the kelp as the currents flow through. We thank you for the shifting sands of the Sahara.

We ask for greater compassion toward the homeless, poor, widows, and children within the confines of our country first, lest we forget them. We ask for your miraculous healing hands to be placed upon those suffering through the many diseases, disorders, and ailments. We ask for truth to replace the deception perpetrated by those in high places. We ask for closed minds to open so all will utilize their intuition when making decisions. We ask for a time where we unite without the hatred, misunderstanding, and greed that divides us. We ask for protection for the defenseless, from the animals that inhabit the lands, mammals of the seas, to the people that are suffering through domestic violence and abuse. We ask for an end to our addictions that separate us from our true path. We ask for a cleansing of our spirits and strength of true knowledge, to replace the negativity we have allowed to remain for too long. For those that are low in spirit, we ask for strength, comfort, and courage be granted to them. We ask for the return of our children that have been abducted and find themselves in modern-day slavery. We ask for justice for the victims and awareness for us all.

We thank you for those warm summer days, as well as the snows of winter, where children play, and families come together to celebrate life around the evening fire. We thank you for the shades of the maple, oak, and weeping willow trees. We thank you for the four seasons that show us that life also goes through its changes. We thank you for those that may come into our lives for a short time to bring insight, and to show us those things that we may have forgotten. We thank you for the precious gift of life and the experience you have granted us. We thank you for the knowledge that even in our darkest hours, you are there when we call upon you. So, it is. So shall it be.

Great Spirit, Almighty Healer, and Creator of all things, with humble hearts we gather to offer our sincere gratitude. We thank you for the sacredness of the circle found throughout your creation; for our orbit around the sun and moon's orbit around the earth; the beauty of the bird's nest; cycle of life from childhood to childhood; the sky that surrounds us; and all mysteries within the universe that surrounds us. We thank you for the clouds that bring the moisture to the lands to allow for growth and purification. We thank you for our daily food and ask for its blessing. We thank you for the water that hydrates our bodies. We thank you for the air that gives us life. We thank you for the clothes on our backs and the shelter that is available to us. We thank you for the precious gift of all life.

We ask for greater understanding toward the many gifts you have bestowed upon us. May we learn to use them properly and for what they are intended for. We ask for healing for our spiritual, mental, and physical health. We ask for integrity and honesty to find its way once again into our hearts. We ask for the veils of secrecy, that have been hidden for so long, to continue to be lifted for the world to see. We ask for hardened hearts to soften; closed eyes to open; clogged ears to loosen; and clouded minds to clear. We ask for greater compassion toward the homeless and the poor. We ask for a greater outpouring of support for those that stand against those that continue to destroy what you have created. We ask for mercy toward those that have joined together to begin to repair the damage against the environment. May your strength, guidance and conviction be granted unto them. We ask for an end to the narcissistic mind and a new beginning in selflessness.

All praise and glory belong to you in all that you have created and overseen. We lift our hearts in love, in reverent fear. We remain watchful for your truth to be revealed; your justice to permeate from the church to all facets of where the darkness has adhered itself. We look forward to more awakened hearts and a better world of peace and compassion. We stand in awe of your majestic universe to the smallest detail that you have engrained in all things. We remain humble by your answering of our prayers. So, it is. So shall it be.

Great Spirit, Almighty Healer, and Creator of all things, it is with humble hearts that we assemble to send many thanks. We thank you for the trees that give us air to breathe, the many herbs and plants to cure ailments and diseases, and the waters that flow from the mountaintops to hydrate our bodies. We thank you for our daily food and ask for its blessing. We thank you for our elders that bring us the necessary wisdom and lessons to aid us along our journey. We thank you for our children that will one day take these and build upon them for future generations. We thank you for the many trials that strengthen our spirits. We thank you for your forgiveness when we stray from our paths.

We ask for continued healing for those that are suffering through diverse diseases, disorders, and ailments. May we better understand that you have provided the cures in the many plants and herbs available. We ask for your comfort and peace for those that may have lost loved ones. For those that have crossed over into the Spirit World, we ask for strength and guidance to be granted. We ask for protection, guidance, and strength to be placed upon those that continue to stand against governments and corporations that threaten to destroy more of your creation. May we return to the old ways where we were better stewards of the land and the animals that are around us. We ask for more hardened hearts to soften and closed eyes to see what we must do to repair the damage we have done to our Earth Mother. We ask for an end to the hatred, racism, greed, and lust for power and materialism that can be found across the four corners. We ask for guidance each day as we journey along our paths. We ask for a greater awakening of spirits that will align with those that will protect your creation and assist those in need.

We thank you for your mercy and forgiveness. We thank you for the knowledge and wisdom that tells us that you create only life, and that all we see, and feel is alive. We thank you for Mother Earth that supplies us with everything that will sustain life. For the greatest gift of life, we thank you. We thank you for all that we see around us as well as that which we cannot. So, it is. So shall it be.

Great Spirit, Almighty Healer, and Creator of all that surrounds us, it is with a humble heart that we unite to offer many thanks. We thank you for the beauty of the butterfly as it flutters about us on a calm sunny day. We thank you for the brilliance of the fireflies during the cool evening hours. For the crawlers that aerate the soil, and the lightning that provides nitrates for growth, we thank you. We thank you for the knowledge we receive when we observe the ant and the bee as they work together to bring miraculous things, so too is our ability when we become organized. We thank you for our thorns, for they keep us from becoming too boastful in life.

We ask for continued and miraculous healing for those that are suffering through afflictions of the spirit, mind, or body. We ask for comfort and peace to be granted for those that have lost loved ones and still grieve their loss. May they be granted knowledge that their loved ones are watching over them now. We ask for the release of those that have been incarcerated for crimes they did not commit. We ask for the protection of all animals that are suffering through abuse, unnecessary slaughter, and trophy hunting. We ask for the veils of secrecy to be lifted and show to all the deception that has been used to control them. We ask for prophesies and dreams to be granted to your children that understand that they are merely vessels, and that miracles are brought to us by you. We ask for an end to the abuse and violence perpetrated against our women and children. We ask for your calling to go out to more awakened spirits so we may have a greater impact on restoring the environment. We ask for greater compassion to be granted to help the poor, homeless and the elderly.

We thank you for our elders that bring us the wisdom of the ancestors and life lessons for the present. May they receive the respect they deserve. We thank you for our children that remind us of innocence and lessons long forgotten. We thank you for our many trials that serve to strengthen our spirit. We thank you for the precious gift of all life. We thank you for your forgiveness, love, patience, and discipline that allows us to be molded into the person you have created. So, it is. So shall it be.

Great Spirit, Almighty Healer, and Creator of all things, it is with humbled hearts that we congregate to offer many thanks. We thank you for the sacred circles found throughout your creation, from the outer expanse of the universe to life cycles and the nests in the trees. We thank you for the rising of the sun each morning as it begins to light our paths and provide sunlight to the plants. We thank you for the clouds that bring the rain to areas of need. We thank you for the rushing waters that flow from the mountaintops to hydrate our bodies. We thank you for our daily food and ask for its blessing. We thank you for the rain forests as they supply us with the air to breathe. We thank you for the dreams and visions given to better prepare us for what lies ahead. We thank you for the sacred spirit that connects us to all living things and to you.

We ask for closed eyes to open so they may see the destruction that is being caused. We ask for greater unity among your people so we may begin the arduous task of repairing what we have nearly destroyed. You have guided this generation to erect a firm foundation for the next to build upon, and we ask for your strength and further guidance to accomplish this for them. We ask for strength, guidance, and courage to stand against those that would further destroy what you have created. We ask for strength when we become surrounded by those that know only negativity in life. We ask for your words to be imparted from our mouths to those that may be sitting on the fence between unbelief and belief. We ask for a time of repose where we can clear our minds and bring back the fire of our spirit. We ask for comfort and guidance also to those that have lost their way. We ask for blessings for those that have great faith in you. We ask for freedom for all that have been imprisoned with false accusations, as well as for those that have found themselves in modern-day slavery. We ask for greater compassion to be shown toward the poor and the homeless across the four corners during this time of great turmoil. We ask for healing for those that have endured violence and abuse in their lives. We ask for protection for those that continue to endure these horrendous acts. We ask for an end to our addictions that keep us from our path.

We thank you for our elders and the lessons they have given. May we continue to honor them with the deepest respect. We thank you for our children that will one day take over and lead your people. We thank you for your many blessings and gifts that you have bestowed upon your children. We thank you for all answered prayers. We thank you for the precious gift of life and the reminder that all life is sacred. We thank you for our families and friends that continue to support us when we are in need. We thank you for our animal friends in nature that show us the true meaning of life and the wisdom that comes when we learn to watch and listen. So, it is. So shall it be.

Great Spirit, Almighty Healer, and Creator of all things, it is with humble hearts that we assemble to offer many thanks. We thank you for swimmers that inhabit the waters from the mountains to the deep seas below. We thank you for the bear, the deer and the wolves that live in the forests. We thank you for the buffalo and horse that roam the plains. We thank you for the fliers that soar in the skies above us. We thank you for all relations that interact with us each day. We thank you for the crawlers that work around in the soil. We thank you for all that we have taken for granted, from the tallest tree to the single grain of sand. We thank you for the sacredness of the ground we walk upon for it holds the blood, sweat, and tears of our ancestors.

We ask for comfort to be afforded for those that are low in spirit. We ask for guidance, strength, and protection for our brothers and sisters that stand against those that continue to destroy what you have created. We ask for an end to the hatred, greed, racism, and lust for power, that has found their way into a world of misunderstanding and selfishness. We ask for veils of secrecy to be lifted, so we begin to understand all that has been controlling us. We ask for a time of peace where all people are truly equal, where no one person holds more power than the next. We ask for an end to the violence and abuse perpetrated against the women and children throughout the four corners. We ask for freedom for those that have been taken from their homes unjustly. We ask for unity throughout Mother Earth so we may begin the long, arduous task of bringing back her beauty, freshness of the skies, and pureness of the waters. We ask for protection for all the defenseless that face grave dangers throughout your creation. We ask for greater compassion and generosity for those that are poor or are homeless on this day.

We thank you for our elders that bring us the wisdom and necessary lessons that will help us along our path. We thank you for our children that will build upon the foundation this generation will leave them. We thank you for the trials we endure that will help to strengthen our spirits. We thank you for your forgiveness when we stray from our path. We thank you for the sacredness of all things you have created, from the vast expanse of the universe to the very core of our Earth Mother. We thank you for the many blessings and gifts you have bestowed upon your children. So, it is. So shall it be.

Great Spirit, Almighty Healer, and Creator of all things great and small, seen and unseen, it is with a humble heart that we unite to offer many thanks. We thank you for answering our faithful prayers. We thank you for the knowledge that you are in control of all things, though we may not understand why certain things happen. We thank you for the Sacred Spirit that walks among us, to guide us along our path. We thank you for new friends and family that bring us the insight we need, handed out in portions, as we continue our journey.

We are ashamed, Adonai, of our continued arrogance and lack of love for ALL life. We have taken your creation that is used to bless us and destroyed it for profit or for trophies. We ask for your mercy and the changing of minds and hearts of those that cannot see through their blindness. We ask for a time when people understand the gifts that you give us to enrich our lives. We ask for forgiveness when we take without replacing, or we hunt for more than we need. We ask for greater love to break the chains that have hardened our hearts and compassion toward all life be found within us. We ask for an end to the hypocrisy that can be found throughout our governments. We ask for clarity of understanding, love, and compassion to enter into our leaders throughout the four corners. Our leaders are elected to unite their people, but unfortunately, they divide us even further. We ask for your intervention to honor the prayers of your people that look to you for unification. We ask for forgiveness when we fail to look to you with honor and faithfulness, and instead trust in the world to handle our problems. May there be a time where we learn to ask for forgiveness and turn from our ways, for our blessings to continue.

We thank you for the rain that comes to areas of need. We thank you for your discipline when we error or disappoint you. We thank you for your mercy and your forgiveness. For your love, compassion, and understanding, we thank you. We thank you for the wisdom and instruction you have given to our ancestors that continue to be passed to each new generation. We thank you for the warnings and prophecies that you have given us. May we remain alert and be watchful during these trying days. So, it is. So shall it be.

reat Spirit, Almighty Healer, and Creator of all things, we unite together with humble hearts to offer many thanks. We thank you for the gift of life, that you have breathed into every living thing. We thank you for the many blessings and gifts you have given us. We thank you for the tranquility we find as we gaze upon the rolling creeks, in the early morning hours, while listening to the songs of the wren and finch. We thank you for the aroma of fresh cut grass, and the sweet smell of the gardenia. We thank you for your love and grace. We thank you for the scent of the salt air, as the ocean waves gently glide along the coastal shores. We thank you for the swaying of the palms and willows.

We have allowed materialistic greed and money to control us. We ask for your forgiveness and guidance. We have polluted the lands, water, and sky and have brought hatred, corruption, and division where we were once united in peace. We ask for a return to an era of peace where all people are truly equal, and we can use the gifts provided to bring back balance to a world that is destroying itself. We ask for strength, guidance, and courage, as we stand against those that would continue to destroy the lands, waters, and skies above. We ask for an end to the corruption, greed, and lust for power and wealth of those that are supposed to serve their people. We ask for an end to the division that continues to keep your people from uniting and fulfilling the prophecies. We ask for the release of all your children that have been incarcerated for crimes they did not commit. We ask for a time for boys to become men and become real fathers to the children they have sired. We ask for hardened hearts to soften and compassion be used to help the poor, homeless, widows, and all that are in need. We ask for guidance each day so we may work toward an era of renewal and heal our Earth Mother. We ask for protection for all that are defenseless against the onslaught of evil that surrounds them. We ask for an end to the wars and hostilities. We are with heavy hearts and are weary of such mindless aggression and wish only unity and balance in an unbalanced world. We ask for protection for the babe in and out of the womb.

We thank you for our many trials as they bring strength to our spirits. We thank you for our elders as they bring us the instruction and wisdom needed to follow our path. We thank you for our children that will build upon the foundation we have set before them. We thank you for our relations that interact with us each day to give us insight into areas of misunderstanding. We thank you for our family and friends that give us the support we need along our journey. So, it is. So shall it be.

Great Spirit, Almighty Healer, and Creator of all things, it is with a humble heart that we unite as one to offer many thanks. We thank you for our daily food and ask for its blessing. We thank you for the friendships we meet along our paths, that bring us the insight and wisdom to aid us along our journey. We thank you for the wisdom and teachings of our ancestors, that have been passed on through the generations. We thank you for our families that bring us support and comfort we need during our trials. We thank you for those trials that serve to strengthen and prepare us for that which lies ahead.

We ask for greater leadership in our governments where all serve their constituents with integrity and honor. We ask for a time where parents become proper caretakers and teachers of integrity to their children. We ask for an end to single parenthood, where fathers or mothers have taken on the hardship and responsibility alone. May we begin to focus upon a full family structure and a strong foundation set for our children. We ask for greater compassion toward widows, children, homeless, and the poor. We ask for a greater outpouring of spirit that will teach us all the proper ways to live our lives, as you commanded us to do in the beginning. May we turn away from the materialistic and technological world that leads to destruction and become focused upon taking great care of the environment, animals, and each other. We ask for our eyes to open and our minds to grasp all that has been hidden for too long. We ask that we become able to discern fact from deception; truth from lies; straight answers from distortions. We ask for a bountiful harvest this year that will bring forth food to feed all that are suffering through hunger, from our own lands to those over the great waters. We ask for an end to all forms of hostility, from domestic violence to wars and skirmishes throughout the four corners.

We thank you for the blessing of living upon this great planet and learning all we need to learn here. We thank you for the warm gentle breezes that flow across grassy meadows. We thank you for the time we spend observing nature, and becoming more enlightened about how much it can teach us. We thank you for the moral compass placed upon our hearts at birth, that serves to give understanding of right and wrong. We thank you for the precious gift of all life, and the knowledge that all lives matter. So, it is. So shall it be.

Great Spirit, Almighty Healer, and Creator of all things, it is with humble hearts that we assemble to bring forth this prayer of requests and praises. We thank you for each new day of life granted to us. We thank you for the signs in the heavens that give us prophecy of future events. We thank you for the beauty of the birch and maple trees during the autumn months. We thank you for the moving waters of the brooks and streams, as well as the rushing of the river currents. We thank you for the rains of purification and relief that come to areas of need. We thank you for the breezes that flow through the meadows and farmlands during the summer months.

Show us, Adonai, the need for patience. Show us all that has been hidden from the people by those in high places, regardless of how horrific it may be. Awaken the minds, eyes, and hearts of those that have lain dormant for too long. Bring forth hidden cures and energies that have also been hidden for the sake of greed. Show us your justice against those in the churches, corporations, and governments that have gone against you, and the people of the world. Bring forth cures for those that are suffering from cancers, diabetes, high and low blood pressure, and pestilence. Show us your glory and might in these coming months that will bring forth a greater spiritual awakening. May those that have been headed for the broad road of destruction turn back toward the narrow path of righteousness. Show us our gifts and how to use them in the way you have planned. Show us your ways.

We long for, and anxiously await, your return and reign. We remain humbled by your works, for you are the Potter and we are the vessels of clay that you have placed the spirit into to do your will. We bow before your power, glory, and omnipotence. For without you, we can do nothing. We are in awe of the meticulousness of each molecule you created, and how it makes up each atom, ultimately leading to wondrous miracles of creation. We marvel at the intensity of the energy that emanates around all things. So, it is. So shall it be.

Great Spirit, Almighty Healer, and Creator of all things, it is with a humble heart that we unify to offer many thanks. We thank you for the many herbs and plants that provide us with cures for our ailments and diseases, and for the nourishment that is given. We thank you for the water that flows from the mountaintops that hydrate our bodies. We thank you for the trees and the rainforests that give us the air to breathe. We thank you for the gentle winds that soothe our spirits and the music it brings. We thank you for the peace that can be found in the nature that surrounds us. We thank you for the wisdom found in the trees and animals that inhabit the forests. We thank you for the early morning stillness of the lakes and oceans reminding us that each day starts anew, and many wondrous things can be accomplished.

We ask for comfort and guidance for those that are low in spirit. We ask for a great revival of spiritual awakening during this time of turmoil and distress. We ask for protection for our animal friends, the bear, the wolf, the horse, the buffalo, the whale, and the dolphin, that are facing grave danger from those that do not understand how precious all life is. We ask for the awaited gathering of those that will begin to protect the animals from those that will hunt for sport. We ask for protection, guidance and strength as we stand against those that willfully destroy more of your creation. We ask for an end to the greed, corruption, lust for power and wealth that is found in our governments. We ask for an era of peace in a world that is weary of war and those in governments that sanction them. We ask for the veils of secrecy to continue to be lifted so the people will begin to understand and make informed decisions. For those that are low in spirit and desperation, we ask for guidance and comfort to be given. We ask for an end to the violence and abuse being suffered by our women and children. We ask for closed eyes to open, hardened hearts to soften, and clogged ears to loosen in a time where unity of the four colors is needed. We ask for an end to the division that separates us and slows down the unity we need to bring back balance to an unbalanced world. We ask for a spiritual revival to overtake the lands covered in desperation and turmoil.

We thank you for our elders that bring us wisdom, life lessons, culture and heritage awareness, and the stories from long ago. We thank you for our children that will take the lessons and wisdom they learn from us, on to the next generation. We thank you for the great expanse of the universe that surrounds us and is the very center of our being. We thank you for the wisdom and spirit that resides in our heart. We thank you for our ancestors that remain with us from the Spirit World to help us during our journey. We thank you for your forgiveness when we stray. We thank you for your love and guidance given to us each day. So, it is. So shall it be.

Great Spirit, Almighty Healer, and Creator of all things, it is with a humble heart that we congregate to offer many thanks. We thank you for the rains that purify and provide growth to the plants and herbs. We thank you for the wondrous flight of the geese as they fly toward the south before the winter months. We thank you for all the two-legged, four-legged, swimmers, fliers, and crawlers throughout each day. We thank you for the mist and dew as dawn begins to appear over the horizon. We thank you for the aroma of the salt air as we near the ocean.

We ask for great healing for those that continue to suffer through afflictions of the spirit, mind, or body. May we learn to use the many plants and herbs you have provided to cure us. We ask for comfort for those that have lost loved ones. We ask for guidance, strength, and courage for those that have crossed over into the next phase of life. We ask for guidance each day as we journey along the path of compassion and peace. We ask for an end to the division among your people that keeps us from uniting together as we should. We are weary from the many wars and ask for an end to all hostilities. We ask for closed eyes to see, clogged ears to open, and hardened hearts to soften toward those that have been misunderstood for so long. We ask for an end to the killing of our brothers the horse, buffalo, wolf, bear, whale, and dolphin. We ask for an end to the trophy hunting that continues to destroy the sacredness of our animal friends. We ask for freedom for all that have been incarcerated for crimes they did not commit.

We thank you for our elders that speak true, teach us present day lessons, and the wisdom of the ancestors. We thank you for our children that continue to show us the innocence and lessons long forgotten. We thank you for friends and family that remain with us to give us support when we are in need. We thank you for your patience, love, guidance, discipline, and comfort. So, it is. So shall it be.

Great Spirit, Almighty Healer, and Creator of all things, it is with a humble heart that we gather to offer our requests, as well as our thankfulness. We thank you for the clouds that gather up the moisture from the oceans and seas and deliver it to areas of need. We thank you for the coolness of the evening and the warmth of the day. We thank you for all the two-legged, four-legged, swimmers, fliers, and crawlers throughout each day. We thank you for the soaring of eagles of the north, and the hawks of the south. We thank you for the rushing waters that flow from the snowcapped mountaintops to the lakes and oceans below. We thank you for the sound of crashing waves upon the rocky shore and the gentleness upon the sand. We thank you for the seasons of bountiful harvest. We thank you for the multi-colored flowers of the plains, and the colors of the autumn leaves.

We ask for greater compassion for those across the four corners that are suffering through homelessness, as well as the poor. We ask for more clinics to help those of our soldiers still suffering from the trauma of wars. We ask that closed doors begin open to all that are looking for work. We ask for the cleansing of our hearts, so we may better understand the messages sent to us. We ask for guidance each day as we journey along the path of compassion and peace. We ask for blessings be given to those that have walked straight along their path. We ask for the understanding of the gifts you have given us, so we may use them for the betterment of all. We ask for an end to the trophy hunting that continues to destroy the sacredness of our animal friends. We ask for freedom for all that have been incarcerated for crimes they did not commit. We ask for protection and eventual freedom for our women and children that have been abducted and abused.

We look to your compassion for the answering of our prayers. We understand that you have granted us the knowledge that you are in control of all things, though we may not understand why or how certain things happen. You have blessed us with the Sacred Spirit that resides within us, to guide us along our path. You have opened the veil of secrets that have brought forth new friends and family that bring us the insight we need, handed out in portions, as we continue our journey. We look forward to new adventures along life's path. So, it is. So shall it be.

reat Spirit, Almighty Healer, and Creator of all things seen and unseen, it is with humble hearts that we unite to offer up many thanks. We thank you for the precious gift of life when we arise each morning. We thank you for the many prayers you have answered during our lives. We thank you for our elders that continue to show us lessons and wisdom of the ancestors. We thank you for our children that have shown us lessons long forgotten and will build upon the foundation set forth by previous generations. We thank you for the sacredness of the circle found throughout your creation, from the vast expanse of the universe to the smallest nest of the flier on Earth. We thank you for the knowledge that even in our most tumultuous storms, there can be beauty and peace, we just need to know where to look.

We ask for protection for the innocent throughout the world. We ask for your comfort, courage, and guidance through days of loneliness, desperation, and indecision. We ask for a swift end to the violence perpetrated by those that have no regard for the sacredness of life. We ask for mercy toward your believers when we stray from our path. We ask for guidance each day as we follow the unique paths you have placed before us. We ask for patience when we want to rush into things without allowing for the right time to arrive. We ask for love to enter the hearts of the unbelievers, and for light to pierce into the darkness that surrounds us. We ask for protection and mercy for those that have chosen to turn away from the materialism and harmful technologies that are leading us down the wrong path, and guide us down the path of nature and compassion. We ask for knowledge toward the dreams and visions that you have given us. We ask for guidance and direction in our search to understand the truth, when we have been subjected to disinformation and deception throughout the years.

We thank you for the crisp morning air as we arise in the morning. We thank you for the food we receive each day and ask for its blessing. For the clean, rushing waters of the mountains that hydrate the bodies of all living things, we thank you. We thank you for the warm tropical breeze as it flows through the palm leaves, and the warm ocean waters. We thank you for our trials and our thorns that serve to strengthen and keep us grounded each day. We thank you for family and friends that support us along our path. We thank you for those that may come into our lives for a short time to bring insight, when we are in need. We thank you for the continued opening of the veil during this time. We thank you for the guidance given to us to accomplish the tasks at hand. So, it is. So shall it be.

reat Spirit, Almighty Healer, and Creator of all things, it is with
humble hearts that we unite to send many thanks. We thank you
for the trees that give us air to breathe, the many herbs and plants to
cure ailments and diseases, and the waters that flow from the mountaintops to
hydrate our bodies. We thank you for our daily food and ask for its blessing.
We thank you for our elders that bring us the necessary wisdom and lessons to
aid us along our journey. We thank you for our children that will one day take
these and build upon them for future generations. We thank you for the many
trials that strengthen our spirits. We thank you for your forgiveness when we
stray from our paths.

We ask for continued healing for those that are suffering through afflictions
of the spirit, mind, or body. May we better understand that you have provided
the cures in the many plants and herbs available. We ask for your comfort and
peace for those that may have lost loved ones. For those that have crossed over
into the Spirit World, we ask for strength and guidance to be granted. We ask
for protection, guidance, and strength to be placed upon those that continue to
stand against governments and corporations that threaten to destroy more of
your creation. May we return to the old ways where we were better stewards of
the land and the animals that are around us. We ask for guidance each day as
we journey along our paths. We ask for a greater awakening of spirits that will
align with those that will protect your creation and assist those in need. We ask
for freedom for those that have been imprisoned without cause, and for those
that have been taken from their homes.

We thank you for your mercy and forgiveness, Father. We thank you for the
knowledge and wisdom that tells us that you create only life, and that all we see,
and feel is alive. We thank you for Mother Earth that supplies us with everything
that will sustain life. We thank you for our relations, families, and friends that
help to strengthen us when we tend to be weary. For the greatest gift of life, we
thank you. We thank you for all that we see around us as well as that which we
cannot. We thank you for the magnificence of the universe around us and all of
its great mysteries. So, it is. So shall it be.

Great Spirit, Almighty Healer, and Creator of all things, it is with a humble heart that we gather to offer many thanks. We thank you for the many herbs and plants that provide us with cures for our ailments and diseases, and for the nourishment that is given. We thank you for the water that flows from the mountaintops that hydrate our bodies. We thank you for the trees and the rainforests that give us the air to breathe. We thank you for the gentle winds that soothes our spirit and the music it brings. We thank you for the peace that can be found in the nature that surrounds us. We thank you for the wisdom found in the trees and animals that inhabit the forests. We thank you for the early morning stillness of the lakes and oceans reminding us that each day starts anew, and many wondrous things can be accomplished.

We ask for comfort and guidance for those that are low in spirit. We ask for a great revival of spiritual awakening during this time of turmoil and distress. We ask for protection for our animal friends, the bear, the wolf, the horse, the buffalo, the whale, and the dolphin that are facing grave danger from those that do not understand how precious all life is. We ask for protection, guidance, and strength as we stand against those that willfully destroy more of your creation. We ask for an end to the greed, corruption, lust for power and wealth that is found in our governments. We ask for an era of peace in a world that is weary of war and the governments that sanction them. We ask for the veils of secrecy be lifted so the people will begin to understand and are able to make informed decisions. For those that are low in spirit and desperation, we ask for guidance and comfort be given. We ask for an end to the division that separates us and slows down the unity we need to bring back balance to an unbalanced world. We ask for the awaited gathering of those that will begin to protect the animals from those that would hunt for sport. We ask for greater awareness toward those that are in need. We ask for doors of opportunity, once closed, to be open to all that need work or housing. We ask for a spiritual revival to overtake the lands covered in desperation and turmoil.

We thank you for our elders that bring us wisdom, life lessons, culture and heritage awareness, and the stories from long ago. We thank you for our children that will take the lessons and wisdom they learn from us, on to the next generation. We thank you for the great expanse of the universe that surrounds us and is the very center of our being. We thank you for the wisdom and spirit that resides in the heart. We thank you for our ancestors that remain with us from the Spirit World to help us during our journey. We thank you for your forgiveness when we stray. We thank you for your love and guidance given to us each day. So, it is. So shall it be.

Great Spirit, Almighty Healer, and Creator of all things seen and unseen, it is with humble hearts that we congregate as one to offer many thanks. We thank you for the knowledge that we have in the last days, and what we do now will determine our fate. We thank you for all the blessings you have given your children, and the gifts to use for those in need. We thank you for the signs of warning that you have shown, leading to this point in time. May we heed your warnings and strengthen ourselves in you.

We have become a world of lawlessness and unbelief, and we ask for your forgiveness. We ask that you teach us each day to always look upon the light and move away from the darkness that serves to consume us. We ask for our addictions to be taken away, so we can focus entirely upon you. We ask for an end to the slaughter of the innocents. We ask instead for a world of peace and true equality toward each other, to do the things we were meant to do from the beginning. We ask for your miraculous healing hands to be placed upon those that are suffering through disease and disorders. For those who are in hospitals that are being operated on, we ask that you guide the hands of the surgeons. We ask for the release of the innocent still imprisoned for crimes they did not commit. For those that are contemplating suicide, we ask for your mercy, guidance, love, and peace.

We thank you for the rising and setting of the sun, that has been with us from the beginning. We thank you for the moon that has watched over us during our slumber for many centuries. We thank you for Mother Earth that has provided us with all the necessities of life. We thank you for the sky as it continues to protect us from the hazards of the space beyond. We thank you for our elders that continue to teach us wisdom, and present-day insight. We thank you for our children that have reminded us of the innocence we once knew. So, it is. So shall it be.

Great Spirit, Almighty Healer, and Creator of all things, it is with a humble heart that we gather and lift our hands to you in thankfulness. We thank you for the soft blankets of snow during the season of slumber. We thank you for the playfulness of the children as they scurry about the outdoors. We thank you for the soft, gentle breeze that caress our cheeks in the early morning hours. We thank you for the beauty of the autumn colors found in the forests. We thank you for the warmth of the summer months. For the season of life, as the seeds begin to germinate, we thank you.

We ask for discernment, so we may make better decisions during these tumultuous days. We ask for courage to stand against the evil that now permeates every facet of life. We ask for patience when we tend to want things instantly in our lives. We ask for understanding that we are to be in constant prayer, in order to fight against the principalities and powers that have come against us. We ask for strength when we become weak; courage when we become afraid; energized when we become weary. We ask for protection for ourselves and for those that lead us. We ask for mercy for those that are unaware of their misdeeds. We ask for cures for our natural and man-made afflictions. We ask for the end of all human and sex trafficking throughout the globe.

We thank you for all answered prayers. We thank you for the winds that flow across the fields of grain. We thank you for the harvest we receive each year. We thank you for our elders that bring us the wisdom and teachings of the ancients. We thank you for the lifeblood of all living things. For the rain that comes to areas of need, we thank you. We thank you for your love, discipline, patience, and guidance each day. So, it is. So shall it be.

G reat Spirit, Almighty Healer, and Creator of all things, it is with a humble heart that we gather to offer many thanks. We thank you for the wren upon the branch as she sends out the melody in the early morning hours. We thank you for those random acts of kindness, that bring joy to our hearts. We thank you for the hummingbird as it hovers over the petal while collecting its nectar. We thank you for the songs of the wrens in the early morning hours. We thank you for the strength of the eagle and the persistence of the hawk.

We ask for a greater awakening of spirits during these days. We ask for an end to bigotry, hatred, greed, and lust for both power and money. We ask for guidance, strength, and courage as we continue along our path. We ask for an era of peace where all people are truly equal, and generosity abounds. We ask for a stronger rising of spirit as we begin to replant, defend the defenseless, and bring back honor and courage to your children. We ask for assistance to be given for those struggling with mental issues. We ask for the opening of doors, where present ones begin to close. We ask for greater compassion be given to those that are aware of those in need. We ask for a bountiful harvest this year for those that till the soil, so they are able to feed the multitudes. We ask for greater understanding of the messages and signs that may be sent to us. We ask for a thorough cleansing of our feet so we may go where we are meant to go; our hands so we may create beauty; our hearts so we may better understand its messages; our eyes so we may behold the glory of your creation; our surroundings, so we may not be diverted into evil.

We thank you for our elders and the wisdom they provide us during our journey. We thank you for their stories of morality. We thank you for our children that will continue to build upon the foundation this generation has erected. We thank you for Mother Earth that gives us the water to hydrate us, food to nourish us, and cures for our ailments. We thank you for the sky that continues to protect us. We thank you for the nature that surrounds us and gives us tranquility in a troubled world. So, it is. So shall it be.

Great Spirit, Almighty Healer, and Creator of all things, it is with humble hearts that we unify to offer our sincere gratitude. We thank you for the sun that rises early to bring us the warmth and the lighting of our path each day. We thank you for the morning mist as it caresses the ground of the valleys near the running water. We thank you for the spring dew that falls from the plants and herbs that give us the cures we need for our afflictions. We thank you for those random acts of kindness that bring joy to our hearts. We thank you for the bees that pollinate the plants and provide us with honey. We thank you for the hummingbird as it hovers over the petal while collecting its nectar. For the flight of the dragonfly over the pond, we thank you. We thank you for the songs of the wrens in the early morning hours. We thank you for the strength of the eagle and the persistence of the hawk. We thank you for the ant, mole, and earthworm that aerate and create new soil.

We ask for discernment where we are better equipped to weed out the misrepresentations and lies that have been used to divide your people. We ask for guidance, strength, and courage as we continue along our path. We ask for guidance, strength, and courage for those that continue to stand against injustice, and the destruction of your creation. We ask for an era of peace where all people are truly equal, and generosity abounds. We ask for an end to homelessness and hunger. We ask for a stronger rising of spirit as we continue to battle principalities and powers in this spiritual warfare. We ask for assistance to be given to those struggling with mental issues. We ask for an end to stereotypes and discrimination. We ask for freedom and an end to modern-day slavery that can be found throughout the four corners. We ask for an end to this present pestilence. We ask for greater compassion to be given to those that are aware of those in need.

All praise and glory belong to you in all that you have created and overseen. We lift our hearts in love, always fearing our Adonai. We stand in awe of your majestic universe to the smallest detail that you have engrained in all things. We remain humbled by your answering of our prayers. So, it is. So shall it be.

Great Spirit, Almighty Healer, and Creator of all things, with humble hearts we congregate as one to offer our thankfulness. We thank you for the sacredness of the circle found throughout all your creation, from the seemingly endless galaxies of the universe, the seasons of our Earth Mother, the bird's nest, and the core of our world. We thank you for answering our prayers from the past, present, and those yet to be. We thank you for the healing powers you have granted to those that are your vessels upon this earth. We thank you for the many blessings and gifts that you have bestowed upon your people that walk in faith. We thank you for the sacredness of the soil, and the knowledge that our bodies were formed from our Earth Mother and one day will return to her. We thank you for the knowledge that our spirit does not end on this plane of life, where we become educated and given a purpose for the present, and that we will move on to the next phase of life when our ailing bodies return.

There are many that have come to us for healing. We ask that you use your vessels to bring miraculous healing to those that are suffering through afflictions of the spirit, mind, or body. May your glory be shown throughout the globe that you are still with us and miracles can still happen for people of faith. We ask for your hands to guide the surgeons that will soon operate on your children. We ask for your strength, comfort, and peace to be granted onto those that need your healing. We ask for greater understanding to those that have not learned of the many herbs and plants that you have created that will heal diseases and disorders. May we soon turn from man-made chemicals and trust in your creation. We ask for protection for our brothers, the animals that face grave danger these days. May your judgement be upon those that wantonly kill for sport, trophies, and abuse. May we grow to understand the animals so we will no longer fear them. We ask for an era where there is peace, a resurgence of Mother Earth's healing, and unconditional love permeates throughout the four corners. We ask for an end to materialistic lust, greed, hatred, and corruption. We ask for your guidance to be granted to more spirits that will soon awaken. We ask for an end to the abuse and violence perpetrated on our women and children.

We thank you for our elders that give us the wisdom of the ancestors and the lessons of the present day. May respect once again be granted unto them as it should. We thank you for our children that have reminded us of lessons long forgotten and the blessings of innocence. We thank you for our daily food and ask for its blessing. We thank you for the water that hydrates the bodies of all living things. We thank you for the wisdom given to us to draw from when we are in need. We thank you for family and friends that support us and give us insight during our journey. We thank you for our ancestors that remain with us to watch over us and protect us. So, it is. So shall it be.

Great Spirit, Almighty Healer, and Creator of all things, with humble hearts we unite to offer many thanks. We thank you for the gentle winds as they flow through the trees and the grassy plains. We thank you for the water that flows from the snowcapped mountains to the ocean below. We thank you for all two-legged, four-legged, swimmers, fliers, and crawlers that inhabit the Earth. We thank you for the clouds that carry the rain from the oceans to areas that have become dry and thirsty. We thank you for our food and ask for its blessing. We thank you for the music from the crickets under the shadow of night, and the fliers that wake us in the early morning hours.

We ask for an end to homelessness and for closed doors of opportunity to open. We ask for a bountiful harvest so all people can be fed. We ask for an end to famine and disease. For those imprisoned for crimes they did not commit, we ask for their release. We ask for an end to the violence and abuse being suffered by our women and children. We ask for forgiveness, Father, for we have caused great destruction to our Earth Mother through pollution, litter, mining, flacking, and strip mining; cut down trees without replanting; poisoned our air; and hunted for sport and trophies. We ask for hardened hearts to soften; closed eyes to open; clogged ears to hear. We ask for veils of secrecy throughout the four corners to be lifted. We ask for protection, guidance, and strength as we stand against injustice and against those that would willingly bring more destruction to your creation. We ask for a change of mindsets in our government, so they may begin to return to a time where our focus was upon you and your blessings. We ask for greater compassion and respect for the sacredness of the unborn.

We thank you for our elders that deserve so much respect. May we teach our children the importance of respecting all things. We thank you for our children that continue to remind us of lessons long forgotten. We thank you for the precious gift of life and the unique paths given. We thank you for your love, forgiveness, correction, and patience. We thank you for the wisdom and knowledge you have gifted us with. So, it is. So shall it be.

reat Spirit, Almighty Healer, and Creator of all things great and small, it is with humble hearts that we come together united to offer up many thanks. We thank you for the swirling snow on a cold winter's day. We thank you for the graceful movement of the wave upon the sandy shore during the spring. For the shade under the canopy of the weeping willow during the hot days of summer, we thank you. We thank you for the beauty of the multi-colored leaves of autumn, as they prepare for the season of slumber. We thank you for the sacredness of the circle found throughout your creation, from the vast expanse of the universe to the core of our Earth Mother.

We thank you for those that come to us for a short time to provide us with much needed insight. We thank you for our trials as they provide us with the wisdom and strength to empower us for that which lies ahead. We thank you for the understanding that to achieve balance, we must take the good with the bad in life, within this dimension. May their lessons strengthen our soul. We thank you for our ancestors and guides that watch over and protect us, during our lives here on this plane of existence. We thank you for the rising of the sun as it reminds us of the precious gift of life. We thank you for the moon as it watches over us during our slumber. We thank you for the sky's protection and Mother Earth's provisioning our bodies with all we need to survive. We thank you for our elders as they show us, through lessons of the present to the wisdom of the past, that we can remain strong and provide this strength to future generations. We thank you for our children as they enjoy playing around the outdoors and will one day find their place in the halls of power. May they be educated in the ways of righteousness.

We thank you for the mists that flow softly down from above during the season of birth and renewal. We thank you for the clouds that gather up the waters of the oceans and bring it to thirsty lands. We thank you for the warm breezes that flow through the fields of grain. For the music heard in the rushing waters, and the winds that caress our cheeks, we thank you. We thank you for the ever-changing universe that surrounds us. We thank you for the spirit of all living things and the uniqueness that abides throughout all your creation. So, it is. So shall it be.

reat Spirit, Almighty Healer, and Creator of all things, it is with humble hearts that we unite to offer many thanks. We thank you for the spirit that dwells within us and in all living things. We thank you for our ancestors that are still with us in spirit, and the wisdom they provide. We thank you for all the two-legged, four-legged, swimmers, fliers and crawlers that surround us. We thank you for the music found in the gentle winds that flow through the trees and the cascading waters. We thank you for the trials we endure that strengthen and prepare us for what lies ahead. We thank you for the many answered prayers.

We ask for an end to the turmoil that has kept your people divided for too long, so we may work toward balance. We ask for an end to such hatred, greed, lust for power and materialism that is found in our governments and corporations, that have filled the hearts of those that have become complacent and naive. We ask for freedom for those that have been abducted or taken from their homes without cause. We ask for protection for your forests, water, plains, and deserts that man has taken parts of your creation without replacing. We ask for strength, guidance, and courage for those that stand against governments that do not protect the lands or honor the treaties they have signed. We ask for guidance each day so we may travel our paths with courage, strong legs and straight eyes. We ask for more compassion to be placed upon the hearts of those that are aware of the homelessness in their cities. We ask for more open doors for them, so they may once again be able to live productive lives.

We thank you for our elders that show us many life lessons and wisdom to carry within us during our journey. May we always endeavor to bring great honor to them. We thank you for our children that continue to teach us innocence and lessons long forgotten. May we provide them with an unbreakable foundation from which they will build on. We thank you for our relations that interact with us during the day that strengthen our spirits. We thank you for the gift of life and the paths you have given us. May we learn to listen intently before we speak and understand that there is strength in silence. We thank you for our food and ask for its blessing. So, it is. So shall it be.

Great Spirit, Almighty Healer, and Creator of all things, great and small, it is with a humbled heart that we come together as one to offer many thanks. We thank you for the knowledge of uniqueness. Just as everyone is unique, so too are each blade of grass, leaf, snowflake, and grain of sand upon the seashore. We thank you for the wisdom that you have placed before us throughout our lives. We thank you for the Sacred Spirit that guides, comforts, grants gifts, and sends up our prayers. We thank you for each trial we endure that strengthens us. We thank you for our thorns that keep us from becoming too boastful and proud. We thank you for your grace that surpasses all understanding.

We ask for calmness in our soul when we are troubled. We ask for discernment when we are indecisive. We ask for a greater outpouring of charity toward those in need. For those that stand against injustice, wherever it may be, we ask for your strength, guidance, and courage to be upon them. We ask for your guidance and patience for those that lead us. We ask for your hedge of protection to be upon us during these tumultuous times. We ask for the healing of our diseases, disorders, and ailments. We ask for humility when we tend to be boastful and proud. We ask for courage, strength and patience when we plant the seeds for your harvest. We ask for protection for our women and children who are suffering through domestic abuse. We ask for peace in a world set on its own destruction. We ask for the release of Leonard Peltier and all that have become political prisoners. We ask for greater compassion toward those that are less fortunate than ourselves. May we begin to treat each other with the respect they deserve.

We thank you for the rain that comes to areas of thirst. We thank you for the wisdom and teachings of our elders. May we once again honor them with the respect they deserve. We thank you for our children that will carry on and improve upon their inheritance. We thank you for our family and friends that continue to give support when we are in need. We thank you for your love, patience, guidance, forgiveness, and discipline. So, it is. So shall it be.

Great Spirit, Almighty Healer, and Creator of all things, it is with humble hearts that we congregate to offer our sincere thankfulness. We thank you for the rising of the sun each morning as it brings light to our paths, warmth, and photosynthesis to the plants. We thank you for the clouds that bring the rain to areas of need. We thank you for the rushing water that flows from the snowcapped mountaintops to hydrate our bodies. We thank you for our daily food and ask for its blessing. We thank you for the rain forests and oceans that supply us with the air to breathe. We thank you for the thunderous sounds of the waterfall emptying into the pool below.

We have done little to change our passive ways and we ask for your forgiveness and guidance, so we may begin to rectify the corruption and evil within the halls of all global governance. We ask for greater unity among your people so we may begin the arduous task of repairing what we have nearly destroyed. You have guided this generation to erect a firm foundation for the next to build upon, and we ask for your strength and further guidance to accomplish more for future generations. We ask for strength and peace, when we become surrounded by those that know only negativity in life. We ask for a time of repose where we can clear our minds and bring back the fire within our spirit. We ask for comfort and guidance also for those that have lost their way. We ask for signs to be given to those that do not believe in your existence. We ask for blessings and protection for those that have great faith in you.

We bow to your glory and omnipotence. We remain watchful for your truth to be revealed; your justice to permeate from the church to all facets of where the darkness has adhered itself. We look forward to more awakened hearts and a better world of peace and compassion. We anxiously await your return and your kingdom to be placed in your holy land. We look forward to walking on the paths of love, light, and tranquility in the coming age. So, it is. So shall it be.

G reat Spirit, Almighty Healer, and Creator of all things, it is with a humble heart that we unify to send up requests alongside our deepest thankfulness. We thank you for the many things you have created here on Mother Earth that we may not see, that serve many purposes. We thank you for those things which surround us that we can see, as well as those we cannot. We thank you for the wisdom and the strong spirit found within us. We thank you for the many visions and dreams you send to your children. We thank you for each new day and the precious gift of all life. We thank you for the protection given during our travels.

We ask for forgiveness when we have not listened to or obeyed your words. We ask for guidance, strength, and courage to move forward and defend the defenseless as we begin to repair the damage we have done. We have littered the lands with our waste; introduced smog into the air we breathe; dumped our trash and plastics in the very lifeblood of all living things; and have scarred Mother Earth with our greed through diverse forms of mining. We ask for guidance and patience, to clean the air we breathe, the waters we drink, and the land we inhabit. We ask for continued healing for those that are suffering through afflictions of the mind, body, or spirit. We ask for a stronger and better education system for our youth, so they may become better prepared for their future.

We thank you for the trees that give us air to breathe, the many herbs and plants for nourishment and cures, and the waters that flow from the mountaintops to hydrate our bodies. We thank you for the sight of the squirrel, as he stores up his food for the Winter months. May we learn to prepare ourselves, as well, for that which lies ahead. We thank you for our elders that bring us the necessary wisdom and lessons to aid us along our journey. We thank you for our children that will one day take these and build upon them for future generations. We thank you for the many trials that strengthen our spirits. We thank you for our thorns, our weaknesses, that prevent us from becoming boastful and proud. So, it is. So shall it be.

reat Spirit, Almighty Healer, and Creator of all things, it is with humble hearts that we unite to send many thanks. We thank you for the trees that give us air to breathe and shelter when we are in need. We thank you for the many herbs and plants that we use to cure ailments and diseases. We thank you for the waters that flow from the mountaintops to hydrate our bodies. We thank you for our elders that bring us the necessary wisdom and lessons to aid us along our journey. We thank you for our children that will one day take these and build upon them for future generations. We thank you for the many trials that strengthen our spirits.

We ask for your comfort and peace for those that may have lost loved ones. For those that have crossed over into the Spirit World, we ask for strength and guidance to be granted. May we return to the old ways where we were better stewards of the land and the animals that are around us. We ask for more hardened hearts to soften and closed eyes to see what we must do to repair the damage we have done to our Earth Mother. We ask for an end to the hatred, deception, racism, greed, and lust for power and materialism that can be found across the four corners. We ask for guidance each day as we journey along our paths. We ask for strength when we are weak; understanding when we are fearful; peace when we are agitated. We ask for a greater awakening of spirits that will align with those that will protect your creation and assist those in need.

We thank you for your mercy and forgiveness. We thank you for the knowledge and wisdom that tells us that you create only life, and that all we see, and feel is alive. We thank you for Mother Earth that supplies us with everything that will sustain life. We thank you for our daily food and ask for its blessing. We thank you for our relations, families, and friends that help to strengthen us when we tend to be weary. For the greatest gift of life, we thank you. We thank you for all that we see around us as well as that which we cannot. We thank you for the magnificence of the universe around us and all of its great mysteries. So, it is. So shall it be.

Great Spirit, Almighty Healer, and Creator of all things, it is with humbled hearts that we unite to offer many thanks. For the clouds that carry the water over long distances to areas that may be in need. We thank you for the music heard in the gentle winds and the rushing waters when we stop to listen. We thank you for the eagle that soars above the storm reminding us of how we should face our obstacles along sacred path. We thank you for allowing us each new day of life.

We ask for forgiveness, when we allow our minds to control our hearts, making us think we know all things. There are times we believe only what our minds tell us and have forgotten the wisdom of the heart. We ask for continued healing for those that are suffering from man-made and natural diseases and disorders. We ask for more of your children to become awakened during this time so we may begin the long struggle of bringing back balance. We ask for an era of peace and tranquility. We ask for freedom for those that have been abducted or taken from their homes without cause. We ask for protection for your forests, tundra, waters, plains, and deserts that man has arrogantly taken without replacing. We ask for strength, guidance, and courage for those that stand against this onslaught, as well as trying to protect their homeland. We ask for a change within governments in all countries that continue to enslave your people. We ask for protection for all the two-legged, four-legged, swimmers, fliers and crawlers that are facing danger.

We thank you for our relations that interact with us during the day that strengthen our spirits. We thank you for the gift of life here and the unique paths you have given us. May we walk them with straight eyes and strong legs. We thank you for all answered prayers. With the wisdom we receive we will learn to be more patient than we are. So, it is. So shall it be.

reat Spirit, Almighty Healer, and Creator of all things, with humble hearts we come together to offer many thanks. We thank you for the calls of praise to you from the wolf and coyote under the moon. We thank you for the swiftness in flight of the eagle and hawk. We thank you for the soft falling snow as the gentle blankets the earth. We thank you for the thundering waterfalls. We thank you for the towering redwoods as they reach toward the heavens. We thank you for the canopy of the willow on a warm summer day. We thank you for the endless stars that dot the heaven above on a clear cloudless night.

We ask for healing for those that are suffering through afflictions of the spirit, mind, or body. We ask for comfort for those that may have lost loved ones recently. We ask for an end to government control over their people throughout the four corners. We ask for an end to wars and hostilities that serve only to bring destruction and death. We ask for an end to corporate greed and materialistic lust for power. We ask instead for an era of peace and true equality for all people, where no one person is greater than the next, and all are content with what they have and where their spirit lies. We ask for a change in how we currently live, which has only brought destruction to your creation. We ask for protection, strength and guidance as we form together to stand against those that would continue to destroy. For those that have heard your call toward regaining balance, we ask for your strength, guidance, and protection for what lies ahead. We ask for an era of healing for our Earth Mother.

We thank you for our elders that bring us the wisdom of the ancestors as well as the lessons of the present. We thank you for our children that will build upon the foundation that has been laid before them. We thank you for the precious gift of life. We thank you for the answering of prayers. We thank you for our daily food and ask for its blessing. We thank you for the sacredness of all life and the spirit that dwells within us. So, it is. So shall it be.

Great Spirit, Almighty Healer, and Creator of all things, it is with a humbled heart that we gather to offer many thanks. We thank you for the many gifts and blessings that you have bestowed upon your children. May we use them for the betterment of all. We thank you for our trials that help to strengthen our spirits. We thank you for our thorns that keep us from becoming boastful and proud. We thank you for your forgiveness when we have strayed from our path and have caused disappointment.

We ask for protection for those that are suffering through domestic violence and abuse. We ask for an ease of tensions and divisions that separate us from our brothers. We ask for an end to environmental abuse and destruction. May we strive to replace all that has been taken from our Earth Mother and to allow time for her to heal. We ask for greater awareness and compassion toward the homeless, widows, children, and the poor. We ask for open doors for those that are seeking work during these years of declining economies. We ask for an end to the materialistic desires that control us. We ask for a time of true equality where no one is more powerful than the next. We ask for an era of peace and tranquility where all four colors are able to unite for the common good. We ask for a greater spiritual awakening during this time of purification so we may begin the arduous task of restoring balance to ourselves, Mother Earth, and strengthening the spirit that dwells in all of us. We ask for an end to all forms of addictions that continue to enslave us. We ask that during our time of the nation's judgement, you look upon and grant protection, comfort, and guidance to the remnant of your children. We ask for protection, guidance and comfort also for your chosen ones.

We thank you for the early morning mist as it floats down from above. We thank you for the morning breeze that caresses our cheeks and brings a sense of peace to our spirit. We thank you for the wisdom that can be found in nature that will find its way into our hearts. We thank you for our ancestors that continue to watch over us from the Spirit World. We thank you for all answered prayers and the many blessings you have bestowed upon your children. We thank you for life and the guidance you provide as we begin a new day. So, it is. So shall it be.

Great Spirit, Almighty Healer, and Creator of all things, it is with humbled hearts that we gather to offer many thanks. We thank you for this time of spiritual awakening that will begin to unite the four colors from across many lands. We thank you for the understanding that all life from the mountaintops to the ocean floors is sacred. We thank you for our daily food and ask for its blessing. For the waters that flow from snowcapped mountains that hydrate our bodies, we thank you. We thank you for the rainforests that provide us with the air to breathe. We thank you for our Earth Mother as she supplies us with the many plants and herbs that serve to both nourish and cure us.

We ask for the release of the walls we build up within ourselves, so we may begin to purify our spirit. For those that are depressed and low in spirit, we ask for comfort and guidance. We ask for guidance and strength for those that are destined to educate their young in the old ways. We ask for comfort for those that have lost loved ones. We ask for strength, guidance, and courage for those that are now on their walk toward the next phase of life. We ask for an end to all violence, greed, hatred, lust, and materialistic desires. We ask instead for an era of peace and equality for all people. We ask for greater compassion and awareness for the homeless and the poor. For those that are in need, we ask that their needs be met with overabundance. We ask for an end to all things that serve to divide us. We ask for forgiveness; we have strayed from our path; have brought destruction to the lands, water, and sky; have taken more than what we have needed; have been envious of our neighbors; and have brought dishonor to ourselves and to you. We ask for the release of all of our brothers and sisters that have been incarcerated purely for political means and bring them home to their family and friends. We ask for an end to the Governments that seek only to impose control upon their citizenry and keep the masses divisive among each other.

We thank you for the rain that falls from the clouds, bringing purification and growth to the lands. We thank you for family and friends that aid us along our journey when they are most needed. We thank you for the coolness of the air, and beauty of the colored leaves. We thank you for our elders that continue to provide wisdom and instruction for present times. We thank you for our children that show us many things we have forgotten over time. We thank you for the answering of prayers. For the sacredness of the circle found in all things, we thank you. We thank you for the precious gift of life. So, it is. So shall it be.

Great Spirit, Almighty Healer, and Creator of all things, it is with a humbled heart that we gather to offer many thanks. We thank you for the warmth of the sun during the day, and the coolness of the moon during the night. We thank you for the many herbs and plants that provide us with cures for our ailments and diseases, and for the nourishment that is given. We thank you for the water that flows from the mountaintops that hydrate our bodies. We thank you for the trees and the rain forests that give us the air to breathe. We thank you for the gentle wind that soothes our spirits and the music it brings. We thank you for the peace that can be found in the nature that surrounds us. We thank you for the Sacred Circle that can be found throughout your creation, from the vastness of the Universe around us, to the very core of our Earth. We thank you for the wisdom, and our moral code, kept within our hearts. We thank you for the cycles of climate and the four seasons. For the rain that comes to areas of arid land, we thank you.

We ask for comfort and guidance for those that are low in spirit. We ask for a great revival of spiritual awakening during this time of turmoil and distress. We ask for protection for our animal friends, the bear, the wolf, the horse, the buffalo, the whale and the dolphin, that are facing grave danger from those that do not understand how precious all life is. We ask for protection, guidance, and strength as we stand against those that willfully destroy more of your creation. We have allowed our government to become a cesspool of iniquity. We ask for an end to the greed, corruption, lust for power and wealth that is found in those very halls. We ask for protection of all sacred lands. We ask for an era of peace in a world that is weary of war and those that sanction them. We ask for the veils of secrecy to continue to be lifted so the people will begin to understand and make informed decisions. We ask for closed eyes to open, hardened hearts to soften, and clogged ears to loosen in a time where unity of the four colors is needed. We ask for an end to the division that separates us, and slows down the unity we need to bring back balance to an unbalanced world. We ask for greater compassion for those less fortunate than ourselves. We ask for a rich bounty of food that will allow all people to be fed.

We thank you for our elders that bring us wisdom, life lessons, culture, heritage awareness, and the stories from long ago. We thank you for our children that will take the lessons and wisdom they learn from us, on to the next generation. We thank you for our ancestors that remain with us from the Spirit World to help us during our journey. We thank you for your forgiveness when we stray. We thank you for your love and guidance given to us each day. We thank you for the many gifts and blessings you have bestowed upon us. We thank you for the knowledge that life is embodied in everything you have created. We thank you for all answered prayers. We thank you for your love, forgiveness, mercy, and blessings. So, it is. So shall it be.

Great Spirit, Almighty Healer, and Creator of all things, with humble hearts we gather to offer many thanks. We thank you for the gift of watching another sunrise. May we use our lives for the purpose you have mandated. We thank you for the Sacred Spirit that guides us on our unique paths through life. We thank you for our elders that teach us lessons for the present, as well as the wisdom of the ancestors. We thank you for our children that will carry the wisdom and lessons they have learned to the next generation. We thank you for our friends and family that remain to bring insight to our lives. We thank you for our lessons learned through your Sacred Word. We thank you for your comfort, strength, and courage as we continue through each day of our lives. We thank you for the beauty of the sunset's reddish hues.

We ask for guidance during times of confusion and misunderstanding. We ask for tranquility when life seems too out of control. We ask for strength when we are low in spirit. We ask for a greater spirit of unity among your children during this time, so we may begin the arduous task of bringing back balance, while raising our vibrations. We ask for an end to the things that continue to divide us. May we learn to love and respect each other, regardless of our differences. We ask for an end to war, in a world where we are deeply weary of the violence and disrespect shown throughout the four corners. We ask for an end to materialistic control and ask for greater freedom to do what must be done. We ask for hardened hearts to soften, closed eyes to open, and veils of secrecy to continue to be lifted. We ask for an end to the hatred, greed, lust for power and money. We ask for greater understanding of all that surrounds us. We ask for guidance, peace, and strength be given to those that have lost hope and are reaching out to others. May we be given your words of encouragement and sympathy to get them through the rough times. We ask for greater compassion for those that are homeless or are struggling.

We thank you for the wisdom found deep within our hearts. We thank you for the mountaintops that give us the rushing pure waters to hydrate us. We thank you for our daily food and ask for its blessing. We thank you for the rain forests that provide us with the air to breathe. We thank you for all the two-legged, four-legged, swimmers, fliers, and crawlers that surround us. We thank you for the wrens and finches that give us their songs early in the morning. We thank you for the ant that shows us the importance of working together. We thank you for the beauty of the hummingbird as it hovers over the petal, and the bees that bring the honey. We thank you for the snowcapped mountains that bring fresh water to the lakes and streams. So, it is. So shall it be.

reat Spirit, Almighty Healer, and Creator of all things, it is with humble hearts we assemble to offer our deepest gratitude. We thank you for the calls of praise to you from the wolf and coyote under the light of the moon. We thank you for the swiftness in flight of the eagle and hawk. We thank you for the swirling wisps of snow as the gentle breeze blows through the trees. We thank you for the thundering waterfalls along the path of the rolling streams. We thank you for the towering sequoias as they reach toward the clouds overhead. For the golden hues rising from the sun in the early morning hours to bring warmth and light, we thank you.

We ask for healing for those that continue to suffer through afflictions of the spirit, mind, or body. We ask for greater compassion during this season for those that are homeless or poor. With winter in full swing, we ask that enough heat and food are provided for them. We ask for an end to government control over their people throughout the four corners. We ask for an end to corporate greed and materialistic lust for power. We ask instead for an era of peace and true equality for all people, where no one person is greater than the next. Strengthen us and show us all your ways, Adonai. We ask for a change in how we currently live, which has only brought destruction to your creation. We ask for protection, strength, and guidance as we form together to stand against those that would continue to destroy. For those that have heard your call toward regaining balance, we ask for your strength, guidance, and protection for what lies ahead. We ask for the awakening of those that remain dormant.

All praise and glory belong to you in all that you have created and overseen. We lift our hearts in love, always fearing our Adonai. We stand in awe of your majestic universe to the smallest detail that you have engrained in all things. We remain humbled by your answering of our prayers. So, it is. So shall it be.

reat Spirit, Almighty Healer, and Creator of all things, it is with
humble hearts that we come to offer many well-deserved thanks. We
thank you for the precious gift of life and the spiritual connection we
all have been awarded. We thank you for our Earth Mother and the knowledge
that she is a living planet, from the highest mountain peak to her very core, that
provides us with all that we need to survive. We thank you for her rainforests that
provide us with the air to breathe. For her blood that rushes from snow-capped
mountains to the valleys below that hydrates the bodies of all living things. We
thank you for all of her herbs and plants that serve to both nourish and provide
cures for our many diseases, disorders and ailments.

We ask for great and miraculous healing for those that are suffering. For those
facing upcoming surgeries, we ask for your strength and comfort to be granted
them. For those surgeons that will be operating, we ask for your hands to guide
them. We ask for an end to the greed and religious zealots that are behind the
wars and hostilities that serve no purpose other than enriching themselves by
conquering lands and people. We ask for an end to materialistic lust that serves
only to enslave and control the masses. We ask instead for a greater spiritual
awakening that will open the eyes that have been closed for so long, soften the
hardened hearts, and unclog the ears that have been listening to the deception
throughout the generations. We ask for these things to not be taken for granted
so that we, as your children, can unite to bring back the land, water, and air to
where they were in the beginning. We ask for your protection, strength and
conviction be given to all your children that stand against those that continue
to bring destruction to your creation, and to those that have heard your call and
will begin to bring back balance to this world in turmoil.

We thank you for our elders that give us the instruction of the present to the
wisdom of the ancestors. May they once again hold the respect they deserve.
We thank you for our children that will soon build upon the foundation set
before them. We thank you for all two-legged, four-legged, swimmers, fliers
and crawlers. We thank you for the many ceremonies you have allowed to help
strengthen our spirit. So, it is. So shall it be.

Great Spirit, Almighty Healer, and Creator of all things, it is with a humbled heart that we gather to offer many thanks. We thank you for that sun that rises early to greet us with warmth and the lighting of our path each day. We thank you for the morning mist as it caresses the ground of the valleys near the running waters. We thank you for the beauty of the waterfall as it gently pushes the water above to the lagoon below. We thank you for the dew that falls from the plants and herbs that give us the cures we need for our afflictions. We thank you for the clean white blanket of snow that covers the soil, preparing it for the upcoming season of birth and rejuvenation. We thank you for the moon that watches over us each night during our slumber. We thank you for your protection during our travels.

We ask for a greater awakening of spirits during these days of chaos and turmoil. We ask for closed eyes to see, hardened hearts to loosen the chains of misinformation and mistrust as we begin the long arduous task of bringing back balance. We ask for an end to bigotry, hatred, greed and lust for both power and money. We ask for your healing hands to be placed upon those that are suffering from afflictions of the spirit, mind, or body. We ask for guidance as we continue along our path. We ask for guidance, strength, and courage for those that continue to stand against injustice and the destruction of your creation. We ask for an end to homelessness and hunger. We ask for a stronger rising of spirit as we prepare to replant, defend the defenseless and bring back honor and courage to your people. We ask for an end to the stereotypes and hatred used to cause division among those that need to unite. We ask for the opening of doors where present ones begin to close. We ask for greater compassion to be given to those that are aware of those in need. We ask for a bountiful harvest for those that till the soil during the season of reaping, so they can feed the multitudes. We ask for rain to come to areas of thirst. We ask for greater understanding of the messages through visions, signs, and dreams that may be sent to us. We ask for a thorough cleansing of our feet so we may go where we are meant to go; our hands so we may create beauty; our hearts so we may better understand its messages; our eyes so we may behold the glory of your creation; our minds so we may not be diverted into evil.

We thank you for our elders and the wisdom they provide us during our journey. We thank you for our children that will continue to build upon the foundation this generation has erected. We thank you for our Earth Mother that gives us the waters to hydrate us, foods to nourish us, and cures for our ailments. We thank you for the sky that continues to protect us. We thank you for the nature that surrounds us and gives us peace in a troubled world. So, it is. So shall it be.

Great Spirit, Almighty Healer, and Creator of all things, it is with humble hearts that we unite to offer up requests alongside our sincere gratitude. We thank you for the sacred circles found throughout your creation; from the outer expanse of the second heaven; life and climate cycles; and the nests in the trees. We thank you for the meticulousness of the inner workings of the human body. We thank you for the wisdom and knowledge we become blessed with when we spend time in nature. We thank you for the rushing waters that flow from the mountaintops to hydrate the bodies of all living things. We thank you for our daily food and ask for its blessing. We thank you for the rain forests as they supply us with the air to breathe. We thank you for the four seasons that remind us of the life span of all living things. We thank you for the loon and duck as they gracefully navigate the ponds and lakes. We thank you for the swimmers of both the fresh and salt waters.

We ask for continued healing for those that are suffering from afflictions of the mind, body, or spirit. We ask for closed eyes to open so they may see the destruction and corruption that exists throughout the world. We are a weary people, Grandfather, of the hatred, greed, and lust for power that permeates from the wealthy and the governments of all nations. We are tired of those of our leaders that do not represent the hearts and minds of their people. We have done little to change this, and ask for your forgiveness and your guidance, so we may live a life of peace and true equality. We ask for truth to come out of the mainstream media, instead of the deception to keep us in fear. We ask for greater unity among your people so we may begin the arduous task of repairing what we have nearly destroyed. You have guided this generation to build a firm foundation for the next to build upon, and we ask for your strength and further guidance to accomplish this. We ask for protection, courage, and strength for those that are now taking a stand to protect the water, land, and air. We ask for strength to our light when we become surrounded by those that know only negativity in life. We ask for a time of repose where we can clear our minds and bring back the fire within our spirit. We ask for comfort and guidance also from those that have lost their way. We ask that you bless our food and drink each day.

We thank you for our elders and the lessons they have given. May we continue to honor them with the deepest respect. We thank you for our children that will one day take over and lead your people. We thank you for your many blessings and gifts that you have bestowed upon your children. We thank you for all answered prayers. We thank you for the precious gift of life and the reminder that all life is sacred. We thank you for our animal friends in nature, that show us the true meaning of life, and the wisdom that comes when we learn to watch and listen. So, it is. So shall it be.

Great Spirit, Almighty Healer, and Creator of all things, it is with a humble heart that we gather to offer many thanks. We thank you for the golden hues of the rising sun each morning. We thank you for the sacred circles found throughout your creation, from the vastness of the universe to the nests of the birds that surround us. We thank you for the seasonal circles that remind us of rejuvenation and regrowth within the cycle. We thank you for the music found in the winds and the rushing waters. We thank you for the moon as it watches over us during our slumber. We thank you for the sky as it protects us both day and night. We thank you for Mother Earth as she supplies us with all we need to survive. We thank you for the sounds of the babbling brook as the waters gracefully glide about and over the rocks. We thank you for the various colors of the wildflowers of the meadows during late Spring.

We ask for strength, courage, and guidance for those that are now meeting their ancestors and loved ones in the Spirit World. For those that have lost loved ones, we ask for comfort to be granted during their grieving process. We ask for protection, courage and strength for all that will stand against the onslaught of destruction to our environment and animals, by those that do not truly understand the sacredness of all life. We ask for hardened hearts to soften; clogged ears to hear; blind eyes to see; and closed minds to open for the truth to be given. We ask for an end to the hatred that seeks to divide your people. We ask for an end to the greed and lust for power that seeks to destroy the spirits of many. We ask for guidance as we continue along our paths so we choose the right direction. We ask for greater compassion to soften the hardened hearts who do not understand the suffering of the homeless and the poor. We ask for teachers to once again teach of the old ways and show us the true path. We ask for a greater awakening and a cleansing of our spirits to prepare us for the arduous task of rebalancing that lies ahead. We ask for a regeneration of the environment and for a strong unity among the four corners. For those that are turning away from civilization and returning to the lands in order to bring back balance in an unbalanced world, we ask for their protection, guidance and strength.

We thank you for our elders and the wisdom of the ancestors they provide. We thank you for the life lessons they advise us of the present. We thank you for our children that remind us of lessons and innocence long forgotten. May we erect for them an unbreakable foundation to build upon for a brighter future. We thank you for all two-legged, four-legged, swimmers, fliers, and crawlers that interact with us and bring us insight and wisdom. We thank you for the strength of the wisdom that lies within our hearts. We thank you for the many trials we endure so they may strengthen our spirit and prepare us for the future. So, it is. So shall it be.

Great Spirit, Almighty Healer, and Creator of all things, it is with humble hearts that we gather to offer many thanks. We thank you for the music of the crickets under the shadow of night, the howling of the wolf as he calls out to the moon, and the rushing waters deep in the forests. We thank you for the winds that flow through the blades of grass, and trees that blow out the old air, to replace it with the new. We thank you for the early morning mist that floats down from above, to provide the earth with moisture necessary for life. We thank you for all the two-legged, four-legged, swimmers, fliers and crawlers that we interact with each day.

We ask for a growing spiritual revival that will soften even the hardest of hearts. We ask for eyes to open that have been closed for too long. May the veils of secrecy at all levels of government, corporations and clubs continue to be lifted. Let us begin a life where no man is greater than the next, and where nothing is done without the knowledge of your people. We ask for protection, courage, and strength to withstand the persecution that surrounds us. We ask for our voices to be heard throughout the four corners where we can begin to teach those that are willing, your ways and the tasks you have given us. We ask for an end to the hatred that has permeated throughout our society and to bring peace to a land where we are suffering. We ask for true equality for all four colors, where we are no longer controlled by greed or materialistic lust. We ask for an era of peace, where we can once again unlock our doors without fear. We ask for an end to the man-made poisons, created in the name of science, and begin to rely upon the herbs and plants you have created for us. We ask for protection for our women and children that are suffering through violence and abuse.

We thank you for our elders that have given us so much while we journeyed along our path. We thank you for our children that remind us of innocence and lessons long forgotten. We thank you for the nature that surrounds us and the tranquility it gives us when we take time out of our daily lives. We thank you for the many trials we encounter that serve to strengthen our spirit. We thank you for the precious gift of life. So, it is. So shall it be.

Great Spirit, Almighty Healer, and Creator of all things, it is with humble hearts that we unite to offer many thanks. We thank you for the sacred circles found throughout your creation; from the outer expanse of the second heaven; life and climate cycles; and the nests in the trees. We thank you for the meticulousness within the human body. We thank you for the wisdom and knowledge we become blessed with when we spend time in nature. We thank you for the rushing waters that flow from the mountaintops to hydrate the bodies of all living things. We thank you for our daily food and ask for its blessing. We thank you for the rain forests as they supply us with the air to breathe. We thank you for the four seasons that remind us of the life span of all living things. We thank you for the loon and duck as they gracefully navigate the ponds and lakes. We thank you for the swimmers of both the fresh and salt waters.

We ask for continued healing for those that are suffering from afflictions of the spirit, mind, or body. We ask for closed eyes to open so they may see the destruction and corruption that exists throughout the world. We are tired of those of our leaders that do not represent the hearts and minds of their people. We have done little to change this, and ask for your forgiveness and your guidance, so we may live a life of peace and true equality. We ask for a greater unity among your people so we may begin the arduous task of repairing what we have nearly destroyed. You have guided this generation to erect a firm foundation for the next to build upon, and we ask for your strength and further guidance to accomplish this. We ask for protection, courage, and strength for those that are now taking a stand to protect the water, land, and air. We ask for strength when we become surrounded by those that know only negativity in life. We ask for a time of repose where we can clear our minds and bring back the fire within our spirit. We ask for comfort and guidance also for those that have lost their way. We ask for protection and healing for those that have endured violence and abuse in their lives.

We thank you for our elders and the lessons they have given. May we continue to honor them with the deepest respect. We thank you for our children that will one day take over and lead your people. We thank you for your many blessings and gifts that you have bestowed upon your children. We thank you for all answered prayers. We thank you for the precious gift of life and the reminder that all life is sacred. We thank you for our animal friends in nature, that show us the true meaning of life, and the wisdom that comes when we learn to watch and listen. So, it is. So shall it be.

reat Spirit, Almighty Healer, and Creator of all things, large and small, seen and unseen. It is with humble hearts that we engage in this prayer of sincere thankfulness. We thank you for the rising of the sun as it stretches out his golden hues over the horizon. We thank you for the rushing streams cascading from the uppermost crests of the mountains to the valleys below. We thank you for the rivers teaming with life under the surface. We thank you for the waterfall that stretches out to the lagoons and rocks below.

We thank you for Mother Earth as she continues to provide us with the cures for every disease and disorders facing us. We thank you for the melodies of the songbirds perched upon the branch, at dawn's light. We thank you for the trees that recycle our exhalations and bring us the necessary oxygen to breathe in. We thank you for the uniqueness of all things, and the knowledge that normality does not exist in nature. We thank you for the many signs and wonders beheld in the heavens above us. We thank you for the sacredness of all life. We thank you for this new age of Aquarius and the upcoming ascension. We thank you for the knowledge that life is far more complex than what we have known.

We thank you for the moon as it continues to keep watch over us during our slumber. We thank you for the four seasons and the four colors. We thank you for the wisdom imparted to us as we continue to travel along our unique paths. We thank you for the story tellers that show morality in the ancestral tales they tell. We thank you for the mysteries of the universe that surrounds us. We thank you for the sky as it provides the clouds that carry the rain to areas of need. So, it is. So shall it be.

reat Spirit, Almighty Healer, and Creator of all things, it is with a humble heart that we give the thanks that you so richly deserve. We thank you, Father, for the blessings you have bestowed upon your children. We thank you for your hedge of protection when we are in need. We thank you for answering our prayers. We thank you for our daily sustenance of food and water and ask for their blessing.

We thank you for the swaying of the leaves of the willow and the maple trees, during the soft summer breeze. We thank you for the brooks and streams as they cascade down from the highest peaks. We thank you for the tranquility found around the waterfall as it pours into the lagoon. For the calmness and serenity of the pond, as the koi swim about, we thank you. We thank you for the beauty shown in uniqueness of the snowflake, during the winter months, as it blankets the hillside. We thank you for the bee, as it pollinates the plants. We thank you for the ant, as it works tirelessly to show us the importance of working together. We thank you for the beauty of the butterfly. We thank you for the music provided by the songbirds in the early morning hours. We thank you for the four seasons that remind us of the cycles of life. We thank you for the signs and wonders that we find in the second heaven.

We thank you for our elders and the wisdom they impart to us. We thank you for our children that will soon inherit all that lies before them. We thank you for friends and family that continue to support us during our journey. We thank you for your patience when we become anxious; your discipline when we have disappointed you; your unconditional love when we stray from our path; and your compassion toward those that believe in you. So, it is. So shall it be.

Great Spirit, Almighty Healer, and Creator of all things, it is with humble hearts that we gather to offer many thanks. We spend so much time going to and from work and home that we rarely take the time to look upon the many blessings we have received in life. We thank you where we can take the time to discover all that we have missed in our daily lives. We thank you for the knowledge that you have given each of us the Sacred Spirit to assist us along our paths. We thank you for those that come to us for a short time to give us the insight we need to move forward. We thank you for our family and friends that remain with us to give support. We thank you for the sense of peace when we perform acts of kindness.

We thank you for the rain that bring moisture to parched lands. We thank you for the denseness of the forests, the grassy plains, and the desert, where we can find beauty in your creation. We thank you for the mists that float from the mountains to the valleys below, bringing along the mists that touch the plants and herbs. We thank you for the warmth of the sun that also brings the lighting of our paths. We thank you for the winds that bring music and wisdom to soothe our troubled hearts. We thank you for the waters that cascade down from the snow-capped peaks, around and over the rocks, and find its way to the lakes and rivers below. We thank you for the rain forests that give us the necessary air to breathe each day. We thank you for our daily food and ask for its blessing. We thank you for the beauty found in the four seasons that also reveals to us the life cycle of all things. We are born, we work as we grow, we relax, and we sleep, and then we move on into the next phase of life to be born again. We thank you for the beauty found among the uniqueness of all things, from the mighty expanse of the universe to each grain of sand upon the ocean floor.

We thank you for our elders that remain to give us the wisdom and lessons we need to build a firm foundation for our children. We thank you for our children that will continue to build upon that foundation, making it strong and lasting for their children. We thank you for the many answered prayers. We thank you for healing those that have looked toward you with humbleness and grace. We thank you for your love, discipline, guidance, strength, and forgiveness. So, it is. So shall it be.

Great Spirit, Almighty Healer, and Creator of all things, it is with a humble heart that we assemble to offer up this prayer of thankfulness. We spend much of our lives in selfishness and looking to the world for our answers, and we thank you for the times of remembrance that we should be looking toward you instead. We thank you for the precious gift of life as we rise each morning from our slumber. We thank you for the unique paths you have set before each of us. May we learn to follow them with strong legs, straight eyes, always looking for your guidance. We thank you for our relations that are before us that help us when we are in need. We thank you for your blessings, love, patience, and forgiveness. We thank you for the many trials we endure along our path that strengthen our spirits. We thank you for the gifts given to those that will use them for the betterment of all. We thank you for our food and ask for its blessing.

We thank you for the rains that come to purify and rejuvenate a thirsty land. We thank you for the rushing waters that flow from the mountaintops to the lakes and oceans below. We thank you for the abundance of life found in the waters, forests, plains, and deserts. We thank you for the mists that blanket the valleys during the early morning hours as Father Sun rises to bring us warmth. We thank you for the four seasons that remind us that all life goes through their cycles. We thank you for the sacred circle that is found throughout your creation, from the vast expanse of the universe to the core of our planet. We thank you for the winds that give us the music to soothe our spirits as it gently caresses our cheeks. We thank you for the trees that recycle the air we breathe. We thank you for the knowledge of the many herbs and plants that give us the cures for our ailments and diseases. We thank you for the water lilies of the pond, and the Koi that swim below.

We thank you for the sacred soil our feet tread upon for they hold the blood, sweat, and tears of our ancestors. We thank you for all answered prayers. We thank you for the wisdom of the ancients that continue to aid us along our path. We thank you for the wisdom you have placed within our hearts. We thank you for the solitude and the lessons we learn when we are at one with the nature that surrounds us. We thank you for those that come into our lives for a short time and for a specific purpose. So, it is. So shall it be.

reat Spirit, Almighty Healer, and Creator of all things, it is with
humble hearts that we gather to offer many thanks. So often we have
taken things for granted and have not opened our eyes to the beauty
that you have created. We send this prayer of thanks for the many blessings and
gifts you have given. We thank you for the lightning that provides the nitrates for
fertile soil. We thank you for the sacredness of the seasonal cycle, the four colors
and the four corners. We thank you for the sacred circles found throughout
the universe, to the bird nests among the trees. We thank you for the trees
that supply us with the air to breathe, by recycling the emissions of our carbon
dioxide. For the rushing waters flowing from the snow-capped mountains that
hydrate our aging bodies, we thank you.

We thank you for the many miracles you have brought to your children. We
thank you for the many herbs and plants that supply us with cures for our
diseases and disorders. We thank you for the precious gift of life. We thank you
for family and friends that support us in our time of need. We thank you for
the spirit that connects all living things. We thank you for the wisdom we find
in our hearts. We thank you for our ancestors that continue to watch over us
and give us the answers we need. We thank you for your strength and guidance
as we stand against those that continue to wantonly destroy your creation. We
thank you for the Sacred Spirit that dwells within your children. May we learn
to listen intently and obey His words. We thank you for our unique paths and
the ability to return when we stray.

We thank you for the early morning dew as it drips from the leaves. For the
budding of new life in the flowers of spring, we thank you. We thank you for
all the two-legged, four-legged, swimmers, fliers and crawlers that interact with
us each day. We thank you for the beauty of the wolf, the grace of the horse, the
power of the bear, and the strength of the eagle. May we take these qualities and
bring back balance to an unbalanced world. We thank you for this season of
slumber that will prepare the land for rebirth and renewal. So, it is. So shall it be.

Great Spirit, Almighty Healer, and Creator of all things, we humble ourselves to give thanks for the many blessings you have granted us. We thank you for the beauty, wisdom, and knowledge we find in nature. We thank you for the sight of the gracefulness of the otter as it swims about the ocean shore. We thank you for the strength of the eagle as it soars above the storm. We thank you for the friendliness and protectiveness of the dolphin. For the majestic gracefulness of the whale, we thank you.

We thank you for the signs you have provided in the heavens. We thank you for the knowledge that we should all learn to focus upon the spirit rather than upon the world. We thank you for the wisdom provided to us through the elders, and for each experience we capture during our lifetime. We thank you for the gifts you provide us through the Sacred Spirit. We thank you for the rain that comes to areas of need. We thank you for the serenity we feel around the waterfall, rushing creeks, and lagoons. We thank you for our children that continue to remind us of innocence and things we have long forgotten.

We thank you for family and friends that give us the support needed during difficult times. We thank you for your love, forgiveness, discipline, and grace. We thank you for answering our prayers. We thank you for our daily sustenance and ask for its blessing. May we never cease to remind ourselves that we should communicate with you each day. We thank you for your guidance and may each step we take be one of prayer. So, it is. So shall it be.

Great Spirit, Almighty Healer, and Creator of all things both seen and unseen, with humble hearts we come together to offer many thanks. Although we live in a world in turmoil and imbalance, we are thankful that there is so much around us that blesses us each day. We thank you for the great rainforests throughout the world that give us the oxygen to breathe in and the carbon dioxide we breathe out that gives back to the trees. We thank you for the many herbs and plants that both nourish and bring us the cures we need. We thank you for blood of our Earth Mother that flows swiftly down to the rivers below that bring our bodies the hydration it needs to survive.

We thank you for the complexity of the connection we have with all living things. As it is with the magnificence of the spider's web, we are thankful for the knowledge that we are all connected with your place in the center. We thank you for the understanding that, although we tend to take things for granted, our actions and words can bring insight and growth to others. We are thankful for the many storms, obstacles and lessons in our lives that bring strength to our spirit for what lies ahead. We thank you for the vast complex Universe that surrounds us and brings wonderment in our spirit when we take the time to observe. We thank you for the many blessings and gifts that you have bestowed upon your children. We thank you for the clouds that give us shade and moisture to thirsty lands.

We thank you for our ancestors that have passed their wisdom, culture, and language through the generations. We thank you for allowing these things to continue to be a part of many of your children within the spectrum of the four colors. We thank you for our elders that bring us the lessons needed for the present and the wisdom from the past. We thank you for our children that will one day soon take their place to lead their people in your ways. We thank you for Mother Earth from which our bodies are created and to which they will ultimately return. We thank you for her soil that holds not only the blood of our ancestors but of their history as well. So, it is. So shall it be.

Great Spirit, Almighty Healer, and Creator of all things that surround us, it is with humble hearts that we gather to offer many thanks. So often we have taken things for granted and have not opened our eyes to the beauty that you have created. We send this prayer of thanks for the many blessings and gifts you have given. We thank you for the storms of life that give us strength to our spirit. We thank you for the sacredness of the seasonal cycle, the four colors and the four corners. We thank you for the sacred circles found throughout the universe to the bird nests among the trees. We thank you for the trees that supply us with the air to breathe. For the rushing waters flowing from the snow-capped mountains that hydrate our aging bodies, we thank you.

We thank you for the many miracles you have brought to your children. We thank you for the many herbs and plants that supply us with cures for our diseases and disorders. We thank you for the precious gift of life. We thank you for our Elders that teach us the importance of life and overcoming the impossible. May we give them the respect they deserve. We thank you for our children that show us the innocence and lessons we have long forgotten. We thank you for the messages given for the hidden truths to be revealed to those that have ears to listen. We thank you for family and friends that support us in our time of need. We thank you for the spirit that connects all living things. We thank you for the wisdom we find in our hearts. We thank you for our ancestors that continue to watch over us and give us the answers we need. We thank you for your forgiveness when we have brought dishonor to you. We thank you for your strength and your guidance as we stand against those that continue to wantonly destroy your creation. We thank you for this awakening period that has brought about the purification process. We thank you for the knowledge of truth given when many are searching for answers.

We thank you for the early morning dew as it drips from the leaves. We thank you for the sun as it send us warmth and light. We thank you for the moon as it watches over us during our slumber. We thank you for the sky as it protects us throughout the day and night. We thank you for Mother Earth as she gives us all we need to survive. We thank you for all two-legged, four-legged, swimmers, fliers, and crawlers that interact with us each day. We thank you for the beauty of the wolf, the grace of the horse, the power of the bear, and the strength of the eagle. May we take these qualities and bring back balance to an unbalanced world. So, it is. So shall it be.

reat Spirit, Almighty Healer, and Creator of all things, it is with a humble heart that we assemble to offer up our thankfulness. We have spent a lot of time sending requests so that often we forget to offer up the thanks for all that you have given us. We thank you for the warmth of the sun each morning as begins to rise over the horizon. We thank you for the moist dew and mists that lightly moisten the soil for the many plants and herbs. We thank you for the fliers that awaken us with the soft music they provide. We thank you for your forgiveness when we stray. We thank you for your love, guidance and strength that enable us to follow our path until our task is complete. We thank you for the Spirit World and the knowledge that life does not end here.

We thank you for the gentle winds flowing through the fields of grain, palms, and leaves. We thank you for the rushing of the waters flowing from the mountaintops to the lakes and oceans below, teaming with swimmers, while hydrating the bodies of all living things. We thank you for the rain forests that give us the recycling of CO_2 to the oxygen we need to breathe. We thank you for all the two-legged, four-legged, swimmers, fliers and crawlers that surround us each day. We thank you for the grassy plains, thick forests and jungles, desolate deserts, and the glaciers. We thank you for our daily food and ask for its blessing. We thank you for the eagle and his reminder that we should live our lives soaring above the many storms. We thank you for our family and friends that help to guide us along our path. We thank you for the moon as it keeps watch over us during our slumber. We thank you for the courage we have, to stand against evil during our time of turmoil. We thank you for the continued unveiling of all that has been hidden throughout the centuries.

We thank you for the sky as it protects us day and night. We thank you for Mother Earth as she nourishes and hydrates us. We thank you for our elders that give us the wisdom and instruction we need along our journey. We thank you for our children that will soon begin building upon the foundation set by the generation before them. We thank you for our ancestors and the wisdom and instruction that they continue to provide. So, it is. So shall it be.

Great Spirit, Almighty Healer, and Creator of all things, it is with humbled hearts that we gather to offer many thanks. So often we have taken things for granted and have not opened our eyes to the beauty that you have created. We send this prayer of thanks for the many blessings and gifts you have given. We thank you for the storms of life that give us strength to our spirit. We thank you for the rain that showers thirsty lands. We thank you for the lightning that provides the nitrates for fertile soil. We thank you for the sacredness of the seasonal cycle, the four colors and the four corners. We thank you for the sacred circles found throughout the universe, to the bird nests among the trees. We thank you for the trees that supply us with the air to breathe, by recycling our carbon dioxide. For the rushing waters flowing from the snow-capped mountains that hydrate our aging bodies, we thank you.

We thank you for the many miracles you have brought to your children. We thank you for the many herbs and plants that supply us with cures for our diseases and disorders. We thank you for the precious gift of life. We thank you for our elders that teach us the importance of life and overcoming the impossible. May we give them the respect they deserve. We thank you for our children that show us the innocence and lessons we have long forgotten. May we erect an unbreakable foundation for them to build upon. We thank you for family and friends that support us in our time of need. We thank you for the spirit that connects all living things. We thank you for the wisdom we find in our hearts. We thank you for our ancestors that continue to watch over us and give us the answers we need. We thank you for your forgiveness when we have brought dishonor to you. We thank you for your strength and your guidance as we stand against those that continue to wantonly destroy your creation. We thank you for the Sacred Spirit that dwells within your children. May we learn to listen intently and obey His words. We thank you for our unique paths and the ability to return when we stray.

We thank you for the early morning dew as it drips from the leaves. For the budding of new life in the flowers of spring, we thank you. We thank you for the sun as it sends us warmth and light. We thank you for the moon as it watches over us during our slumber. We thank you for the sky as it protects us throughout the day and night. We thank you for the earth as it gives us all we need to survive. We thank you for all the two-legged, four-legged, swimmers, fliers and crawlers that interact with us each day. We thank you for the beauty of the wolf, the grace of the horse, the power of the bear, and the strength of the eagle. May we take these qualities and bring back balance to an unbalanced world. We thank you for the upcoming season of slumber that will prepare the land for rebirth and renewal. So, it is. So shall it be.

Great Spirit, Almighty Healer, and Creator of all things, great and small. It is with humble hearts that we unite to offer many thanks. We thank you for the soft cool breeze of the morning air, that caresses our cheeks. We thank you for the germination of the seed as it begins the new life of the plant. We thank you for the rains that come to areas of great thirst. We thank you for the rising of the sun as it begins to bring warmth and light to the land.

We thank you for the morning dew as it drips from the plants. We thank you for the morning mist as it softly touches the soil. For the cascading waters from the mountaintops to the valleys, and oceans below, we thank you. We thank you for the gentle winds that blow through the fields of grain. We thank you for the music of the songbirds, as they sing their songs. We thank you for the trees that provide us with the air we breathe. We thank you for the aerators of the soil, and the pollinators above. We thank you for our brothers, the two-legged, four-legged, swimmer, flier and crawler upon the lands and waters. We thank you for the playfulness of the newborn during the spring season. We thank you for the serenity of the koi ponds, and the calmness of the lake waters in the early morning.

We thank you for the warmth of the summer winds, as children begin to frolic in the secluded swimming holes. We thank you for the fields of grain that will ultimately feed your people. We thank you for the sound of the flute when it is played in the canyons and hillsides. We thank you for our children that continue to remind us of the innocence we have forgotten. We thank you for our elders that take the time to help guide us. We thank you for our family and friends that give support and comfort during our trying times. We thank you for your patience, understanding, redemption, and guidance each day. May we forever learn to bring back our focus toward you, and away from the world. So, it is. So shall it be.

Great Spirit, Almighty Healer, and Creator of all things, it is with a humble heart that we assemble to offer up this prayer of thankfulness. We spend much of our lives in selfishness and looking to the world for our answers, and we thank you for the times of remembrance that we should be looking toward you instead. We thank you for the precious gift of life as we rise each morning from our slumber. We thank you for the unique paths you have set before each of us. May we learn to follow them with strong legs, straight eyes, always looking for your guidance. We thank you for our relations that are before us that help us when we are in need. We thank you for your blessings, love, patience, and forgiveness. We thank you for the many trials we endure along our path that strengthen our spirits. We thank you for the gifts given to those that will use them for the betterment of all. We thank you for our food and ask for its blessing.

We thank you for the rains that come to purify and rejuvenate a thirsty land. We thank you for the rushing waters that flow from the mountaintops to the lakes and oceans below. We thank you for the abundance of life found in the waters, forests, plains, and deserts. We thank you for the mists that blanket the valleys during the early morning hours as the sun rises to bring us warmth. We thank you for the four seasons that remind us that all life goes through their cycles. We thank you for the sacred circle that is found throughout your creation, from the vast expanse of the universe to the core of our planet. We thank you for the winds that give us the music to soothe our spirits as it gently caresses our cheeks. We thank you for the trees that recycle the air we breathe. We thank you for the knowledge of the many herbs and plants that give us the cures for our ailments and diseases. We thank you for the water lilies of the pond, and the Koi that swim below.

We thank you for the sacred soil our feet tread upon for they hold the blood, sweat, and tears of our ancestors. We thank you for all answered prayers. We thank you for the wisdom of the ancients that continue to aid us along our path. We thank you for the wisdom you have placed within our hearts. We thank you for the solitude and the lessons we learn when we are at one with the nature that surrounds us. We thank you for those that come into our lives for a short time and for a specific purpose. So, it is. So shall it be.

Great Spirit, Almighty Healer, and Creator of all things great and small, we humble ourselves to give thanks for the many blessings you have granted us. We thank you for the rising of the golden hue of the sun each morning as it reminds us of the blessing of another day of life. We thank you for the beauty, wisdom and knowledge we find in nature. We thank you for the sight of the gracefulness of the otter as it swims about the ocean shore. We thank you for the strength of the eagle as it soars above the storm. We thank you for the friendliness and protectiveness of the dolphin. For the majestic gracefulness of the whale, we thank you.

We thank you for the signs you have provided in the heavens. We thank you for the knowledge that we should all learn to focus upon heavenly things rather than upon the world. We thank you for the wisdom provided to us through the elders, and for each experience we capture during our lifetime. We thank you for the gifts you provide us through the Sacred Spirit. We thank you for the rains that come to areas of need. We thank you for the serenity we feel around the waterfall, rushing creeks, and lagoons. We thank you for our children that continue to remind us of things we have long forgotten.

We thank you for family and friends that give us the support needed during difficult times. We thank you for the knowledge that the scriptures provide us with truth and ways to live our daily lives. We thank you for your love, forgiveness, discipline, and grace. We thank you for the answering of our prayers. We thank you for our daily sustenance and ask for its blessing. May we never cease to remind ourselves that we should communicate with you each day. We thank you for the reddish hues of the setting Sun each evening. So, it is. So shall it be.

G reat Spirit, Almighty Healer, and Creator of all things seen and unseen, it is with humble hearts that we unite to offer up this prayer of our sincere gratitude. We thank you for the awakening of spirits. We thank you for the lifting of veils that have shown the deception perpetrated against us over the many years. We thank you for the guidance you are showing to the awakened, of what to prepare for in the future. May more dormant spirits be awakened during this turbulent time. We thank you for the knowledge that we should no longer focus upon the world, but upon you instead. We thank you for those that have shown the greatest love of all, that of laying down their lives to continue to allow our freedom. We thank you for those that may have left us and moved into your loving embrace, leaving behind their wisdom, strength, and love that will continue for generations to come.

We thank you for the uniqueness of all things, from each star in the universe; each snowflake settling upon the ground; and each tiny grain of sand along the shore. We thank you for the spirit given to all living things and the knowledge that we are all connected. We thank you for the sacredness of the circle found throughout your creation, from the vast expanse of the universe to the very core of our planet. We thank you for the knowledge and wisdom the Sacred Spirit imparts to us. We thank you for the song of the morning dove in the morning; the flight of the hawk and raven during the day; and the music of the cricket during the evening hours. We thank you for all two-legged, four-legged, swimmers, fliers, and crawlers. We thank you for the wisdom found in nature and the fruit it bears. We thank you for the new friends and families that you have shown us and the blessings they bring forth.

We thank you for our elders that remain to give us the wisdom and lessons needed from the past and present. We thank you for our children that will carry on these lessons far into the future when our bodies return to the ground. We thank you for all that come to us for a short time to provide insight when we are in need. We thank you for your love, guidance, discipline, and forgiveness. So, it is. So, shall it be.

Great Spirit, Almighty Healer, and Creator of all things, it is with humbled hearts that we assemble to offer up this prayer of sincere thankfulness. We thank you for the trials we come across on this day that will strengthen our spirits. We thank you for the coolness of the early morning air as the songs from the fliers rise to awaken us. We thank you for the gentle winds that have taken out the stagnation and replaced it with that of fresher air. We thank you for the rains that have come to areas of thirst to give nourishment and richness to the soil. We thank you for the lightning that supplies nitrates to the ground we plow for the growth of our fruits and grains. For the bees that pollinate the flowers and bring us the sweetness of the honey, we thank you. We thank you for the photosynthesis of the sunlight that brings energy and color to the plants and herbs.

We thank you for the many blessings and gifts that you have blessed us with. May we learn to use them for the betterment of all. We thank you for giving us the many plants and herbs to give us nourishment and cures for all diseases and disorders. May we understand their benefits and use them to cure our aging bodies. We thank you for our family and friends that have remained with us this day, to provide support. We thank you for the guidance you send so we may follow our path with strong legs and straight eyes. We thank you for our elders that have given us tools we need along our journey. May we honor them with great respect. We thank you for our children that will carry the lessons and wisdom on to the next generation. We thank you for the Sacred Spirit that guides, consoles, and directs us in our daily lives. We thank you for our many trials that allow us to overcome and strengthen our soul. We thank you for our thorns that keep us from becoming too proud or boastful. We thank you for the knowledge that we should be compassionate and meek in our daily lives. We thank you for your patience when we stumble and fall.

We thank you for the music that accompanies the coolness of the evening air, from the crawlers and our brother the wolf as he howls over the land. We thank you for the vastness of the universe that surrounds us and all the mysteries it holds. We thank you for all your creation of those things we can behold, and those we are unable to see. We thank you for your forgiveness, love, and guidance this day. We thank you for the answering of prayers. So, it is. So, shall it be.

Great Spirit, Almighty Healer, and Creator of all things, it is with humbled hearts that we assemble to offer up our sincerest thankfulness. We spend so much time being disassociated with our spirit and you that we rarely find the time to give you the thanks you deserve. We thank you for your light during our darkest hours. We thank you for the comfort you give us when we are in despair. For new opportunities after other doors have closed, we give thanks. We thank you for times of solitude and rebalance when we can step away from concrete jungles and spend time in nature. We thank you for the healing you bring when we are suffering. We thank you for the many blessings and gifts you have bestowed upon us. We thank you for the precious gift of life.

We thank you for the holy ground we tread upon each day, as it holds the blood and history of our ancestors. We thank you for the oneness we sense when we lay upon our Mother Earth and being at one with her. We thank you for the wisdom we find in the trees when we clear our minds and learn to listen. We thank you for the rushing waters flowing from snowcapped mountains, the moisture of the leaves and plants during the early morning hours. We thank you for the clouds that bring us rain and snow to provide moisture to the soil, the shade of the willow we are given during the warmest of days. We thank you for the beauty we find in nature. We thank you for the multicolored leaves of the forests during their time of preparation toward the season of slumber. We thank you for the winds that blow across the grassy plains. We thank you for the lightning that provides nitrates to the soil and allows for growth. We thank you for the deer, bear, wolf, beaver, and otters found in the forest. We thank you for the viper, roadrunner, coyote, and spider found in the desert. We thank you for the lion, hyena, elephant, and giraffe of the savannah. We thank you for the tiger, jaguar, leopard, and monkey found in the jungle. For the many endless species of swimmers found in the waters, we thank you. We thank you for our daily food and ask for its blessing. We thank you for the songs of the wren, mockingbird, and the whippoorwill.

We thank you for our elders that remind us of lessons of the past as well as the present. We thank you for our children that remind us of innocence and lessons long forgotten. We thank you for family and friends that continue to be with us during our journey to provide support. We thank you for friends that may be with us for a brief time to give us necessary wisdom and support. We thank you for the endless expanse of the universe that surrounds us. We thank you for the many trials we endure that strengthen our spirit. We thank you for our answered prayers and the understanding that all things have a purpose and a reason. So, it is. So shall it be.

Great Spirit, Almighty Healer, and Creator of all things both seen and unseen, it is with humbled hearts that we gather to offer up many thanks. For the towering rocky gray and green cliffs overlooking the glass-like lake below, we thank you. We thank you for the cascading streams tapering downward to the thunderous waterfall below. We thank you for the plush green forests of ferns, trees, and moss upon the moist ground under its canopy. We thank you for the diverse colors of the Autumn leaves.

We thank you for the rain that comes to arid and parched lands. We thank you for the life found in the deserts painted in brown, green and red. We thank you for the trees, from the Joshua to the Redwood. We thank you for the aroma of the cedar and pine. We thank you for the cool morning air as the Sun begins its assent, reminding us of the gift of another day of life. We thank you for the wildflowers of the plains on a warm summer day. We thank you for the fresh new buds of Spring as they begin to bloom. We thank you for the countless rows of grain and corn of the farmlands. For the diverseness of life under the ocean surface, we thank you.

We thank you for all two-legged, four-legged, swimmers, fliers, and crawlers. We thank you for the playfulness of the child, that will one day learn to become leaders as adults. We thank you for our elders that continue to provide wisdom, counseling and direction to those who wish to learn. We thank you for the storytellers that bring us life lessons in the morals of their stories. We thank you for our daily food and ask for its blessing. We thank you for the lifeblood of all living things. We thank you for our basic needs in life. We, above all, thank you for your love, patience, discipline, comfort, and teachings. So, it is. So shall it be.

Great Spirit, Almighty Healer, and Creator of all things, it is with a humble heart that we gather to offer many thanks. We have spent much time sending requests that we often forget to offer the thanks for all that you have given us. We send this prayer to thank you, Father, for the many things that have been bestowed upon us. We thank you for the rising of the sun each morning as it lights up our paths and provides assistance for growth. We thank you for the moist dew and mist that moistens the soil and the many plants and herbs. We thank you for the majestic mountains and the beauty of their snowcapped peaks.

We thank you for the gentle winds that give us wisdom and music when we take the time to listen. We thank you for the rushing of the waters, teaming with swimmers, flowing from the mountaintop to the lakes and oceans below and hydrating our bodies. We thank you for the rainforests that give us the air to breathe. We thank you for the grassy plains, thick forests, jungles, desolate deserts, and the glaciers of the north. We thank you for our daily food and ask for its blessing. We thank you for the eagle and his reminder that we should live our lives soaring above the many storms. We thank you for the cool evening breeze as it gently caresses our cheeks. We thank you for our family and friends that help to guide us along our path. We thank you for the moon as it keeps watch over us during our slumber. We thank you for the many crawlers that send their music throughout the lands under the shadow of darkness.

We thank you for the sky as it protects us day and night. We thank you for Mother Earth as she nourishes, hydrates, and provides us with the cures we need to survive. We thank you for our ancestors and the wisdom and instruction that they continue to provide. We thank you for the sacredness of the soil we tread upon, for it holds the blood, sweat, and tears of our ancestors. We thank you for your forgiveness when we stray. We thank you for your love, guidance, and strength that enable us to continue our path until our task is complete. We thank you for the Spirit World and the knowledge that life does not end here. So, it is. So shall it be.

G reat Spirit, Almighty Healer, and Creator of all things seen and unseen, it is with a humble heart that we unite to offer many thanks. We thank you for the many signs and wonders shown above. We thank you for the knowledge that you are still in control of the present and future. We thank you for the peace and tranquility we find in nature, away from the turmoil and destruction around us. We thank you for those that you have brought forward to continue teaching that which has been hidden for too long. We thank you for the wisdom within our hearts. We thank you for those that have placed themselves in danger to free the innocent.

We thank you for the many answered prayers of healing of the past, present and future. We thank you for those that come to us in our lives for a short time to provide the insight we need. For the many trials we have endured, we thank you for the strength you provide, and the knowledge that they are to prepare us for that which lies ahead. We thank you for our family and friends that give us the support we need. We thank you for all the two-legged, four-legged, swimmers, fliers, and crawlers that interact with us each day. For the sky that keeps us safe from harmful radiation of space, we thank you. We thank you for Mother Earth that provides us with hydration, nourishment, and cures to our aging bodies. We thank you for the plants and animals that give us the clothing and nutrition necessary to survive. For the trees that provide us with the air to breathe and the shelter we reside in. We thank you for our daily food and ask for its blessing. We thank you for the knowledge that all things have a purpose. We also thank you for the knowledge that those things that have been in secret are now being revealed.

We thank you for your forgiveness when we disappointed you. We thank you for your love even when we may have turned away from you. We thank you for your blessings when you have found favor with us, and your discipline when you have not. We thank you for the many gifts given. May we use them as we should to glorify you. We thank you for giving us strength when we are weak, courage when we are afraid, and comfort when we are in pain. So, it is. So shall it be.

Great Spirit, Almighty Healer, and Creator of all things, it is with humble hearts that we unite to offer a prayer of thanks. We thank you for the trials we come across on this day that will strengthen our spirits. We thank you for the coolness of the early morning and the songs from the fliers that rise to awaken us. We thank you for the coolness of the winter air and the drifting snow, as the breeze gently caresses its blanket of white. We thank you for the moisture that has come to areas of thirst. We thank you for the lightning of the summer storm that supplies nitrates to the soil. We thank you for the rain of the spring season bringing birth and rejuvenation to the land and animals.

We thank you for the many blessings and gifts that you have blessed us with. May we learn to use them to help those in need. We thank you for giving us the many plants and herbs to give us nourishment and cures for all diseases and disorders. May we understand their benefits and use them correctly to cure our aging bodies. We thank you for our family and friends that have remained with us this day, to provide support. We thank you for the guidance you send us so we may follow our path with strength and straight eyes. We thank you for our elders that have given us tools we need along our journey. May we honor them with great respect. We thank you for our children that will carry the lessons and wisdom on to the next generation. We thank you for the wisdom found deep within our hearts. We thank you for the serenity we find when we step out of the denseness of our concrete jungles and into nature where we belong. We thank you for our daily food and ask for its blessing. We thank you for the sacred spirit given to all living things. We thank you for the rainbow and its adherence to your covenant.

We thank you for the music that accompanies the coolness of the evening air, from the crawlers and our brother the wolf as he howls over the land. We thank you for our relations that have come to provide us with insight and wisdom to help us along our journey. We thank you for the vastness of the universe that surrounds us and all the mysteries it holds. We thank you for your forgiveness, love, and guidance on this day. We thank you for the answering of prayers. So, it is. So shall it be.

Great Spirit, Almighty Healer, and Creator of all things, it is with a humble heart that we gather to offer many thanks. We have spent much time sending requests that we often forget to offer the thankfulness for all that you have given us. We send this prayer to thank you for the many blessings and gifts that have been bestowed upon us. We thank you for the moist dew and mist that moisten the soil and the many plants and herbs. We thank you for the majestic mountains and the beauty of their snowcapped peaks. We thank you for the clouds above that bring the rain, snow, and shade during the day. We thank you for the beauty of the wildflowers that flourish in the meadows and plains. We thank you for the beauty of the leaves of the forests as they change to the orange, red and purple hues of the autumn season. We thank you for the calmness of the water in the early morning hours.

We thank you for the gentle winds that give us wisdom and music when we take the time to listen. We thank you for the rushing of the water, teaming with swimmers, flowing from the mountaintops to the lake and ocean below and hydrating all living things. We thank you for the rainforests that give us the air to breathe. We thank you for all the two-legged, four-legged, swimmers, fliers and crawlers that surround us each day. We thank you for the grassy plains, thick forests and jungles, desolate deserts, and the tundra of the north. We thank you for our daily food and ask for its blessing. We thank you for the cool evening breeze as it caresses our cheeks. We thank you for the many crawlers that send their music throughout the lands under the shadow of darkness. We thank you for the sounds of the wolf and coyote calls during the midnight hour. We thank you for the courage we have, to stand against evil during our time of turmoil. We thank you for your signs of warning that we may understand the importance of preparation. We thank you for the Sacred Spirit within us as He teaches, guides, and grants us the gifts needed.

We thank you for the dawn of each new day. We thank you for Mother Earth as she nourishes, hydrates, and provides us with the cures we need to survive. We thank you for our elders that give us the wisdom and instruction we need along our journey. We thank you for our children that will soon begin building upon the foundation set by the generation before them. We thank you for the sacredness of the soil we tread upon, for it holds the history and blood of our ancestors. We thank you for your forgiveness when we stray. We thank you for your love, guidance, and strength that enable us to continue our path until our task is complete. We thank you for the Spirit World and the knowledge that life does not end here. So, it is. So shall it be.

Great Spirit, Almighty Healer, and Creator of all things great and small, it is with humbled hearts that we join to offer up our sincere thankfulness. We thank you for those times where we can discover all that we have overlooked in our daily lives. We thank you for the knowledge that you have given each of us, and the guides that assist us, along our paths. We thank you for our family and friends that remain with us to give support. We thank you for the Sacred Spirit, sent to reside within us, bringing comfort and guidance each day. We thank you for those that are willing to selflessly give of themselves to help others. For those showing everyday acts of kindness, we thank you. We thank you for all first responders, care givers, and law enforcement. We thank you for these times where good overcomes evil, if only for a short time, as we continue to engage them in our spiritual battle. May we ever remain optimistic knowing that in the end, your light will eradicate the darkness.

We thank you for the rains that bring moisture to areas that are in need. We thank you for the denseness of the forests, the grassy plains, and the desert, where we can find beauty throughout your creation. We thank you for the mists that float from the mountains to the valleys below, bringing along the moisture that caresses the plants and herbs. We thank you for Grandfather sun as he brings warmth and the lighting of our paths. We thank you for the cool morning breeze that gently caresses our skin. We thank you for the waters that cascade down from the snow-capped peaks, around and over the rocks and driftwood, ultimately maneuvering its way to the lakes and rivers below. We thank you for the four seasons, that also represent the life cycle of all things. We thank you for nature's way of regenerating when given enough time. We thank you for the ever-changing climate that also goes through its cycles.

We thank you for our days of celebration and comradery felt among each of us, regardless of our differences. We thank you for our elders that remain, to give us the wisdom and lessons we need to build a firm foundation for our children. We thank you for our children that will continue to build upon that foundation, making it strong and lasting for their children. We thank you for the many answered prayers. We thank you for healing those that have looked toward you with humbleness and grace. We thank you for your love, discipline, guidance, strength, and forgiveness. We thank you for our daily food and ask for its blessing. We thank you for each new dawn we have the privilege to awaken to. So, it is. So shall it be.

Great Spirit, Almighty Healer, and Creator of all things, seen and unseen. It is with humble hearts that we gather this day to offer the many thanks you so deserve. We thank you for our daily food and ask for its blessing. We thank you for the waters from the snow-capped mountains, that cascade down to the lakes and oceans below, in which we can hydrate the bodies of all living things. We thank you for the gentleness of the early morning breeze, as the sun rises to bring warmth and growth. We thank you for the flight of the many fliers throughout the four corners. We thank you for those times when we are in nature, understanding that all living things, from the plants to the animals, need pure water to survive. We thank you for the gracefulness of the waves as they gently caress the sandy shore.

We thank you for all two-legged, four-legged, swimmers, fliers, and crawlers upon the lands. We thank you for the air we receive from the trees, as we give them the carbon dioxide they need. We thank you for the beauty of the butterfly emerging from the cocoon, to the hummingbird as it hovers to receive his nectar. We thank you for the bees that pollinate the plants and assist in bringing us a healthy environment. We thank you for the ants that work tirelessly to aerate the soil each day. For the warmth of the summer to the coolness of the winter, we thank you. We thank you for fields of grain that will feed the people across the great waters, as well as here in our homeland. We thank you for the multitudes and diverseness of the swimmers in the ocean waters. We thank you for the oak, birch, and maple leaves in magnificent colors during the autumn season, as well as the soft snow flurries of the winter months.

We thank you for the knowledge you allow us to receive, so we may marvel at the perfection of your creation. We thank you for the stars above so that we may see the signs you give us. We thank you for our elders, and our children. We thank you for family and friends that support and defend us. We thank you for those that serve to keep us safe. We thank you for your Word and the wisdom found within its pages. So, it is. So shall it be.

G reat Spirit, Almighty Healer, and Creator of all things, it is with a humbled heart that we come together to offer many thanks. We have spent much time sending requests, that often we forget to offer up the thanks for all that you have given us. We send this prayer to thank you, Father, of the many things that we may have overlooked which you have bestowed upon us. We thank you for the rising of the sun each morning as it lights up our paths and helps with growth. We thank you for the moist dew and mists that moisten the soil for the many plants and herbs. We thank you for the fliers that awaken us with the soft music they provide. We thank you for the beauty of the spring flowers and the fruit found on the trees and vines. We thank you for the autumn leaves nestled upon the ground. We thank you for the laughter of our children at play.

We thank you for the gentle winds flowing through the grain stalks, palms, and trees. We thank you for the rushing of the waters flowing from the mountaintops to the lakes and oceans below, teaming with swimmers, while hydrating the bodies of all living things. We thank you for the rain forests that give us the recycling of CO2 to the air we breathe. We thank you for all the two-legged, four-legged, swimmers, fliers and crawlers that surround us each day. We thank you for the grassy plains, thick forests and jungles, desolate deserts and the glaciers. We thank you for our daily food and ask for its blessing. We thank you for the eagle and his reminder that we should live our lives soaring above the many storms. We thank you for our family and friends that help to guide us along our path. We thank you for the moon as it keeps watch over us during our slumber. We thank you for the courage we have, to stand against evil during our time of turmoil. We thank you for the music of the songbirds each morning.

We thank you for the sky as it protects us day and night. We thank you for the Earth as it nourishes and hydrates us. We thank you for our elders that give us the wisdom and instruction we need along our journey. We thank you for our children that will soon begin building upon the foundation set by the generation before them. We thank you for our ancestors and the wisdom and instruction that they continue to provide. We thank you for your forgiveness when we stray. We thank you for your love, guidance and strength that enable us to follow our path until our task is complete. We thank you for the Spirit World and the knowledge that life does not end here. So, it is. So shall it be.

reat Spirit, Almighty Healer, and Creator of all things that surround us, it is with humble hearts that we gather to offer up this prayer of gratitude. So often we have overlooked and taken things for granted and have not opened our eyes to the beauty that you have created. We thank you for the many blessings and gifts you have given. We thank you for the storms of life that give us strength to our spirit. We thank you for the rains that shower thirsty lands. We thank you for the lightning that provides the nitrates for fertile soil. We thank you for the sacredness of the seasonal cycle, the four colors and the four corners. We thank you for the sacred circles found from throughout the universe, to the bird nests among the trees. We thank you for the trees and plants that supply us with the air to breathe. For the rushing waters flowing from the snow-capped mountains that hydrate our aging bodies, we thank you. We thank you for the circle of life and all that you have created. We thank you for the flower as it begins to bloom. We thank you for the fruit of the vine, bush, and tree. For the knowledge found in nature, we thank you.

We thank you for the many miracles you have brought to your children. We thank you for the many herbs and plants that supply us with cures for our afflictions. We thank you for the precious gift of life you have blessed us with. We thank you for the rising of the sun each morning to its setting in the evening. We thank you for the vibrant colors of both the sunrise and sunset. We thank you for our elders that teach us the importance of life and overcoming the impossible. May we give them the respect they deserve. We thank you for our children that show us the innocence and lessons we have long forgotten. May we erect an unbreakable foundation for our children to build upon. We thank you for family and friends that support us in our time of need. May we endeavor to overcome the dysfunction of previous generations and break the cycles. We thank you for the spirit that connects all living things. We thank you for the wisdom we find in our hearts. We thank you for our ancestors that continue to watch over us and give us the answers we need. We thank you for your forgiveness when we have brought dishonor to you. We thank you for your strength and your guidance as we stand against those that continue to wantonly destroy your creation. We thank you for the gifts given through the Sacred Spirit. May we use them as they are intended.

We thank you for the early morning dew as it drips from the leaves. We thank you for the sun as it sends us warmth and light. We thank you for the moon as it watches over us during our slumber. We thank you for the atmosphere that surrounds us as it protects us throughout the day and night. We thank you for the beauty of the hidden grottos. We thank you for Mother Earth as she gives us all we need to survive. We thank you for all two-legged, four-legged, swimmers, fliers, and crawlers that interact with us each day. We thank you for the beauty of the whale, the grace of the dolphin, the power of the bear, the persistence of the hawk, and the strength of the eagle. May we take these qualities and bring back balance to an unbalanced world. So, it is. So shall it be.

Poems

The Child in Me

Dennis Binns

When I was a child,
I spoke as a child,
I loved as a child,
I learned as a child,
I discovered beauty as a child.
As I grew older,
The child went away.

I no longer spoke as a child,
I no longer loved as a child,
I no longer learned as a child,
I no longer discovered beauty as a child.
Now that I am old,
The child in me returned.

Water's Journey

Dennis Binns

Of rock-faced mountains,
I am born.
Looking upon the sun,
As I begin to melt away.

Slowly gathering understanding,
As I descend to the valleys and plains.
I quickly begin to find my way around,
The many obstacles coming before me.

I dance upon the rocks,
Glide around the driftwood,
As I gracefully find my way.
Over and under I travel.

I forge new paths,
Along my journey.
Down the slope,
I seek new directions.

Through many trials,
I endure to move forward.
Until I find my way,
To the great expanse.

I have lived a long life.
Long before you knew me.
I am your lifeblood.
From me comes wisdom.

Tranquility

Dennis Binns

For a long time, I have been walking and seeing nothing.
I have lived in the small towns, big cities, deserts, swamp lands,
trying to find that special something.
It is not until I have heard God's calling,
Do I find pleasure and sense of purpose.
I have found His song and it has kept me from falling.
I now sit at ocean's edge,
I am at peace.

Be the Light

What usage does light have? Is it not to expose or brighten? If we are to be the light of the world, then we are to not only brighten the lives of others through positivity, but to also expose those things that are hidden in darkness.

If we are sitting back in our own worldly desires of everyday life, without either emitting the light or exposing the darkness, are we being that light we are supposed to be? Are we to just sit back and wait for others to do the work, or are we to actually begin to bring that light to all?

We must remember that faith without works is dead. That means if we decide to sit back and wait, then we are not performing the work needed. Is that not being lukewarm in our faith? If we see something that is evil or dark, should we not say something?

People that refuse to be light like to place monikers on those that actually are out there doing the work of faith. It is time where we all need to bring up the positive things and remove the negative in our lives. Imagine a world where evil no longer exists.

Finding Truth in Religion

Most of us have concluded that all of what we have been taught, or heard of, has not been completely factual. Often, it has been a part of deep deception. There are things that have been drummed into our heads that anything other than that would be immediately thought of as blasphemy, in some cases.

Let us take for example, the biblical scriptures. We do know that there were scrolls found dating back to around the time of Yahusha (Jesus) that are not found in the present-day biblical text. Have you ever wondered why? If you had not heard, the Vatican was raided back in October of 2017, and aside from the horrors found underneath, there were ancient scrolls and a complete bible found.

As I've stated before, in biblical numerology, the number 7 is perfection and completion. Most bibles we have in our homes are around 66 books, give or take. Mine has 86. Scrolls were found in Qumran some time ago that now make up the Lost and Rejected Scriptures. We won't get into why the missing 711 (or so) books were canonized or thrown out, at this point. Sufficed to say that it was done intentionally for some reason.

But let us ponder over a particular point in the scriptures. Most, if not all but one, Apostle wrote, or had been written of, one of these omitted scrolls. We may ask ourselves why Judas Iscariot had his own book, if he were the one that betrayed Yahusha?

The Vatican, which has been hiding all these complete religious texts, in recent days, has been found to be eviler that previously believed. These evil things, I will not get into, but we all will be made aware of sometime soon. I would personally label them the New Babylon. But I digress. What if instead the betrayer was the one Apostle that did not have a book written, at least to my knowledge? That one Apostle that became the first Pope of the Roman Catholic Church. The same Apostle that denied Yahusha three times after His capture by the Roman guards.

How much of the hidden texts will be made available? And how much will be made clear of what the facts truly are? I'm certain it's going to be quite a shock to most people.

Free Will

Free-will is a way for us to determine a course of action. We can either go left, or right, for instance. In it resides concepts of moral responsibility, praise, guilt, sin, and other judgments. We each determine our own course, or path, in life. No one, or thing, can make those choices for us. Therefore, the Creator gave us this gift. We remain autonomous in our own lives. We can be sovereign if we choose.

Now, if the Creator gifted this to us, then there is no one, or thing, that can make decisions for us, unless we allow that. Permission must be granted by us if we are to have someone else make those choices. The Sacred Spirit also does not choose for us unless we allow it.

Man can therefore, as he does, make decisions without our knowledge. We have seen this over and over throughout history. Like all things there is duality. There is an opposite reaction to any action taken. And that reaction will affect others, since we are all connected. If free-will is taken away from us, then the Creator's judgment will ultimately come into action against the perpetrator.

Lies

A lie is a lie. It shouldn't matter about the intention, it is still detrimental to the mind, body, and soul. Allow me to expound upon that further. There is the lie to hide something, the "white" lie to keep others from becoming disheartened, and then there are lies that are malicious in nature.

Lying, in any form, tends to build up in our subconscious mind, which acts as sort of a hard drive in the brain. Every action, thought, observation, and yes, every lie is stored. It does not get erased.

There are emotions that are attached to each lie. Hatred and fear are most prevalent. The longer we hide these emotions, the more they build up. And we have seen, the more they build, the more likely an eruption of emotions will manifest. And the longer the suppression the lower the vibrating energy within the body accumulates.

It is best to stop the lies, and let the truth prevail. Truth is love, which is higher positive vibration. While lies have the opposite effect. We must all learn to be transparent, honorable, and wise. Live our lives in a truthful manner and keep our energy at a higher plane. If situations come up where we think we need to lie, don't. Let the emotion and the truth come out. Who knows? You may be helping the other person consciously.

Life and Purpose

We are all unique individuals with unique experiences and beliefs. We each have our own paths that we chose to travel on. We choose each life to experience those things that we have yet to learn, as well as those that we failed to understand before.

All living things have a spirit and are connected to the Creator of all things, or Source, as some would call Him. While being connected, we experience the entire gamut of emotions that life has thrown at us. Some we have learned from, some not. Those that we have not, we will return in another life to experience again. Life, therefore, is an institution of learning.

We all go through this, in our own specific and unique path. And yet, some try to convert others to our path. I would question why we feel the need to do that. It is best to understand our own path and leave others to theirs. Yes, some of our thoughts and actions will affect others, but it should resonate with everyone to sense. If it does, then it is something that is gained. But nothing should be forced upon another.

To be as a child, in my way of thinking, is to question. This is how children learn, is it not? Not only do they question, but they also mimic. What parent doesn't want their child to grow? What parent that has such unconditional love not want that for their children? Allow yourselves to move beyond the framework of what have been taught. It is your responsibility to learn your own experiences and truths.

Because we all experience life differently, that connection we have would eventually affect us upon each ascension we experience, in my humble opinion. Some of us have been around for centuries, and some are new to this. But we all have that one thing in common. We chose to learn those things that allow us to grow toward ascension to the next phase. Nothing that the Creator has thrown at us isn't done without a reason. Remember, all things have a purpose. Nothing is coincidence.

Love vs Hate

Allegorically speaking, fighting fire with fire only brings more fire. To douse the fire, one must use the proper agent to fight it. So it is in life, we cannot fight hatred, discrimination, or stereotypes by adding to it. Only love can douse these things. If one allows themself to add to the fire, it only serves to grip their hearts and harden it.

If someone is negative towards you, do not add negativity to that which is already present. Either we need to walk away, or we discuss the issue calmly. We need to strive to love everyone no matter the cost. We do not understand why they may hate; we have not lived their life. But if you douse the fire, you will be blessed. Pray for your enemies that they may learn to love too.

As mundane as the cliche is, love does conquer all. It has loosened hardened hearts and brought peace and miracles to those that have let go of the hatred. If one wishes to depart from your life, allow them to do that. They may have only been a part of your life for a brief time to bring you a message or insight into your life. Do not restrain them through negative acts. Focus on your life, your spirit, and your purpose.

Meaning of Life

What if I were to tell you that the meaning of life is that of learning? Everyone learns at different rates through unique paths. Not one person follows the same path as another, but we are all connected.

Could it be that through all our trials, our biggest goal is to learn not only to love, but to learn what love is. This is something we all must learn in our own way. In this life, there is duality. Love and hate exist here. Which means that evil exists because some have faltered in their lesson.

But on the other side, evil does not exist. It is only love. If the Creator is within each of us, then we are a part of the Creator. Our souls live through many lifetimes, many dimensions, and densities, all to learn new things. And all those lessons we learn are recorded in what some call the Akashic Records, or Book of Life.

What one person learns; another will learn at some other point along their path. Here on Earth, people like Hitler, Genghis Khan, and Napoleon faltered in their learning. But when they passed, their soul returned to love. They then will have moved back to learn how to love before they can progress forward in their journey.

We can learn a lot about ourselves and what is on the other side by listening to those that have near death experiences. I don't think there are enough people that bother to do that. Dying is nothing to fear, for example. It is merely a transition to the next stage. Our souls are eternal.

Nature or Technology

If we read in Genesis, we know that we were formed from the earth. All elements within the earth are within us. I suspect all living things have many of the same elements within them, as well. We are all connected. What happens to one, eventually happens to all.

The earth has healing powers. Many of the indigenous can attest to this. This is why parents, when I was growing up, allowed children to play in the mud and dirt. It built up our immune systems. And if we are a part of the earth, then we too can heal, naturally.

We never really needed pharmaceuticals, in my opinion. What we needed was either to understand how to heal ourselves, or to determine which herbs and plants of the earth would aid in our healing process. Through the centuries we have lost sight of this.

We now are entering into a new phase of life, a new era. Much of what we have gone through has been a lifetime of lessons learned. We all are unique and learn things at different rates. We all will awaken to the new reality at some point. Some have already awakened.

The Hopi people have drawings of the life cycle painted upon their rocks that show that we are coming upon a choice we all must make. One of understanding and living as one with the earth. The other of leaving that mentality and gravitating toward pharmaceuticals and technology. According to these human lifespans, those that travel the path of technology will ultimately destroy themselves, while the other path will continue forward.

I personally do not really know with certainty if this is true, but I tend to lean toward the natural. Either way, we are at a point where we need to learn to meditate on the life we wish to live. We all should be seeking truth now more than ever.

Near Death Experiences

If you are afraid of death, I would suggest you listen to those that have had near-death experiences. Your eyes definitely will be opened. There is nothing to fear. From what I have heard, it is of unconditional love in a different realm. A blissful place where we can manifest anything and be with family members. Anything we wish, we can create. We all have already been there before.

Our life on Earth was done by request in order to learn new things. We have reincarnated several lifetimes, in different places, different worlds, and galaxies. The dimensions we travel through in each incarnation are endless. Each planet, and its inhabitants, will continue ascending through densities.

Are there angels or other souls that reincarnate for a specific purpose? Yes. We all have our own purpose. However, since we are all unique, we will have our own purpose. Some of us are here to prepare others for possible future ascensions by raising vibrations. I don't believe, however, that the human mind now could ever really grasp the vast amount of knowledge available, while we are living in this 3D world.

If you are interested in knowing what the other side is like, I would suggest listening to Anita Moorjani or her website AnitaMoorjani.com. She's been there and speaks about a vast array of subjects on this.

Other Worldly Inhabitants

They have been around for centuries. Starseeds and ET's have lived alongside of us without our knowledge. Some of us have been incarnated during this time to prepare things for humanity. There is a reason why Starseeds, or "old souls," have incarnated, or reincarnated (whether one chooses to believe of not) at this moment in history.

It is said that the Atlanteans and Lumerians came from the stars and were destroyed when they tried to enslave the world. Their technology was far superior to anything mankind had known. Philosophers of Greece have spoken of them, but to this day, no one has been able to find any remnant of them.

And what of the ancient drawings and statues of ancient Egypt? Many displaying non-humans that lived and ruled them. Pharaohs of the time with elongated skulls are said to be ET's. Maybe it's time mankind came to terms that they've been with us for centuries. Even Enoch talked of the Watchers in more depth than Genesis. Maybe we should understand that in this ever-expanding universe, Earth is not the only planet that has life.

How can they stay hidden among us? Some may be humanoid, while others can shapeshift. Yeshua himself, was known to shapeshift after his ascension. Those of our elite forces, like Rangers possibly, have battled some of these beings underground. It is said that the royal family of the UK are shapeshifters and have been documented by eyewitnesses of their reptilian features.

With this being said, it is time for us all to break free of what has been hidden by darkness and look behind the veil. This world, as I see it, is headed for a new age. One without the rulers and governments of old and ascending toward an era of a different governance that moves us from enslavement to freedom. ET's will always be around. I believe more benevolent races will be assisting us as we move forward. But they cannot interfere in a developing society.

Our Purpose

To everything there is a purpose. The Creator does not create without knowing what He is doing. Sometimes we take so much for granted that we do not truly look at the purpose of things that surround us. It is the purpose of the ant to work together with other ants to aerate the soil and build a mound. It is the purpose of the bee to pollinate the plants to promote growth. Such it is with all things. If we take time to go out away from the cities and towns and observe nature in their natural habitat, we will become more understanding of the purpose of the four-legged, swimmers, fliers, and crawlers.

Many question what their purpose is in life. Life is given to us here for us to learn. We learn to make the correct decisions through the many trials we endure. We learn to become more compassionate toward those that are struggling to survive. Sometimes, the Creator will send messengers to us to keep us focused upon the right path. We choose to either ignore or obey these messages. He allows us free will, but always gives us a way back to the right path.

There is a purpose to this life we live today. And so, it will be when we move into the next age. But the things we hope for will not come about until the Creator passes judgement on this age, as He has in the previous ages. I firmly believe that this land will once again be given back to the indigenous people in the next age. For it is the indigenous people that have understood more fully the purpose of all things and how to educate others the importance of taking care of His creation.

Political Correctness

I think political correctness has gone too far in this country, and is part of the problem we have today. It was good when it first started, in that we became more aware of other's feelings. But today, people have taken it so far that we end up walking on the proverbial eggshells so we don't offend anyone.

We had backbones years ago, but now it appears we maneuver around like jellyfish. We were able to laugh at ourselves, now we are not. Some people just take things a bit too seriously these days, and everything has become offensive.

It is good to think of the feelings of others, just as it is for us to look at ourselves and be able to laugh at some of our errors. If we hold it all in, it feeds into our subconscious. We need to remember that we are children of God. When he breathed life into us, He also gave us His emotions. Laughter is an emotion.

Let our intention never be to offend anyone. But let's be real, in that we know whatever we do or say, someone is going to be offended. That's okay because we should not allow that to ruin our day. Let your intent be one of compassion. But don't allow others to dictate how you live your life.

Power in Words and Actions

We must always keep in mind that our words and our actions have strength and are powerful. We are all connected within the cosmic web of life. What one says, thinks, and does affects the whole. If we walk in the spirit, we are setting an example for others to follow. And if we are leading in that regard, then we are all spiritual leaders. Our thoughts and actions (works) produce future movements.

It is in the mind of a spiritual leader to bring peace and tranquility into the hearts and minds of those in need. We do not hate, we love. We do not condemn, we forgive. We understand that the Creator oversees all things. Do we question? Or, do we understand that, though we may not like certain things, there is a reason and a purpose for them. And if there is a purpose, then coincidence becomes a word that is made up to bring into question the actions or spoken words of the present.

Do not hate your enemies. Love them and pray for them. They are lost and need to find the right path. To hate, for a spiritual leader, is to go against everything we stand for. We lead, we love, we bring comfort to those that may be struggling. We provide the positive vibration in our actions, thoughts, and spoken words that help raise up others through selflessness. We then become the light that is spoken of in scriptures.

Now, I do not profess that the scriptures, in its current form, have not been manipulated by man. The unbeliever will do his/her best to deceive and lead astray those that rely upon the Creator. We can say that the Sacred Spirit guides those that translate from the ancient language, but the Spirit does not guide those that refuse to listen and follow the teachings of the divine. So, with that in mind, we should use our discernment and intuition, through meditation and prayer, to answer the questions we may have, as well as bringing into our hearts the lessons of truth.

Always remember the golden rule. Do unto others as you would have them do unto you. That rule alone, if people would hold close to it, is the very foundation of peace. Do those simple things, those small acts of kindness, to bring about the change this world so desperately needs. Keep your focus on the Creator and not so much on the world. We cannot serve two masters. Either we love the Creator, or we love the world. And, what has the world done for you lately?

Reincarnation

"Just as man is appointed to die once, and after
that to face judgment," - Hebrews 9:27

What is man? Is he not of the flesh? The flesh is made from the ground and will decompose back into the ground after death. But we are eternal in spirit. The spirit is genderless. The spirit never dies. The spirit can reincarnate into another human being.

"10The disciples asked Him, "Why then do the scribes say that Elijah must come first?"

11Jesus replied, "Elijah does indeed come, and he will restore all things. 12But I tell you that Elijah has already come, and they did not recognize him, but have done to him whatever they wished. In the same way, the Son of Man will suffer at their hands." - Matthew 17:10-12

It was the spirit of Elijah that was within John the Baptist, just as there is a spirit within us that does not die. Many theologians will argue this, but this comes to me in spirit. And it is the Sacred Spirit that I listen to most. Man is not perfect and at times will either manipulate or deceive the masses so that they believe his/her words.

Religion and Spirituality

We, as humans, incarnate into this life not knowing anything really, other than a sense of spirituality, of some form or other. I know many do not believe in reincarnation, and I respect that. However, I have found during my studies that it is highly probable. I believe I've mentioned that a time or two.

Although we may not know anything about past lives we may have had, some occurrences that have come in dreams or flashbacks of memory. Some may go through life not knowing. But if we come here with a purpose, then nothing is coincidental. And if there is a purpose, then at some point along our journey, we may experience it without realizing that we are performing it.

Since we are all unique, but connected spiritually to all things, then we should know that whatever we do in life will affect the whole. I don't believe the Creator of all things created death. I believe all things have life. If this is true, and I believe it is, then everything we see is a living entity. Maybe then we should start looking at life a bit differently and respecting all things.

Knowing that, through our faith, life continues spiritually after our bodies return to the earth. Where then would our spirits go? To heaven for eternity, or are there more ventures for us to encounter? Will we return to where we were, or move on to other worlds and civilizations?

Personally, I believe in a karmic cycle, and that we go through this to learn what we have missed in a previous life. And will continue through each life until all that is learned eventually breaks us free. I don't, however, believe all beings go through this cycle. I believe angelic beings can incarnate for a purpose and may not have to venture into this. Their purpose may be quite different than ours. Whatever the process is, it exists as a learning tool. Probably the best example of higher learning than what we are used to.

I also believe in the grand scheme of things, that the Creator did not create all the billions of stars and galaxies with only one small planet to have life on. I believe there are thousands, if not millions, of entities out there, and possibly here on Earth, that exist. But one will never really know unless he/she decides to climb out of the proverbial box and seek truth. We may even start studying the scriptures differently instead of skimming over the verses.

Sacredness of the Circle

Everything that God has ordained moves in circles (cycles) as we perceive through knowledge gained. The bird makes its nest in circular patterns; the orbit of the earth in relation to the sun; the rise and fall of the sun and moon upon the earth. The oceans are filled with the waters flowing down from the mountains are again lifted by the clouds to bring moisture once again to the highest peaks. All done in a cycle.

Man could not correctly navigate through the ocean waters at night if not for the relation of the stars to the earth. The seasons are cyclic in nature and never cease. The stars also appear overhead in cycles, of which we can see the signs of the zodiac, at certain times of the year. If truly researched, we will note the climate itself also runs in cycles. All things from past to present have been repeated. The spirits of old still claim their spot in current events. There is nothing new that we have not encountered before, just different actors on the stage.

Just as it reads in Ecclesiastes 1:9 "What has been will be again, what has been done will be done again; there is nothing new under the sun."

Spiritual Reality

Think of life as an onion of sorts. Not everything is as you see it with the naked eye. There are things hidden under each layer you peel off. When we say we are battling powers and principalities, we refer to those things that we cannot see. We also cannot see the deception perpetrated against us.

You'd be surprised at all that has remained hidden from us, from our history to the present day. Many churches, to this day, are subjected to a contract they signed with the government. It is called the 501(c)3. This contract was designed to keep the churches from speaking about anything political. This was only a small part of the deception.

We live in a time where good is bad, and bad is good. But we are also beginning to see much of what has been hidden. I firmly believe that so far, we have only just touched the surface. God told us In Matthew 10:26 "So do not be afraid of them. For nothing is concealed that will not be uncovered, or hidden that will not be made known." We are at that time now.

The main message to take from this is that we all should forget all we have been taught in the past, refresh our minds, pray for truth to be revealed, and for guidance.

Truth or Deception

The trouble with history is that it's only as good as the people who write it down. Even the bible wasn't completely written until several hundred years after the death of Yeshua. Which gives me pause as to how much is true and how much is deception. How can one really know the truth about historical events if nothing is written about it during that time period?

I would suppose the best way is to go within and search through spirit. But we can still be deceived by spirits posing as some spirit we call upon. Which is why we are to be testing the spirits. Seek the facts, as you know them. If they are not of God, they will expose themselves. Who was Yeshua? Was He the Son of Yahweh?

Learn to meditate if you have not done so in life. Yeshua, and the rest of the Essenes, practiced this daily. How do I know? By going to spirit. I have also come to find out that past life regression, if done correctly, gives us truthful insight on what went on historically, through the past lives of others. Dolores Cannon wrote and practiced this for several years, and the spirit has shown me that her writings were accurate. But you will need to discover these things yourself.

We cannot completely rely upon written manuscripts if we do not know when they were written and if they were during the historical period of the focus.

Uniqueness

Let no one exalt themselves above anyone else. We should all remain humble lest we fall into the trap. To think we are more important than anyone else is being boastful and proud. There should not be anyone above us or below us. We are all children of the Creator. We all bleed the same and are spiritual beings enclosed in a fleshly body. There is only one that is above all, and that is Elohim.

The only mentor we should have is the Holy Spirit that guides, comforts, teaches, and gives us the gifts to use. No man can do for us that which we need most. We should never look up to those, like celebrities and politicians, that wish only to be above everyone else.

Be thankful therefore, that we have been blessed to awaken each day knowing that we have the power of the Holy Spirit within us that guides us and comforts us. If we keep the Creator in our thoughts and prayers each day, He will not forsake us. We are all unique, no one person is the same as another. We all have unique paths to follow.

Be the light amid the darkness that surrounds us. Follow His ways, His teachings, and His love for all. There are hard times ahead, but be strong and overcome the world, as Yeshua overcame.

Unrepentance and Judgment

If a nation or a people remain unrepentant, judgement continues to fall upon them. The Creator oversees all things. He created the good and the bad, as it is written. A repentant soul WILL be judged whether it be here on earth or on that Day of Judgement we all will go through.

If a nation remains unrepentant, He will send judgement. He will give us leaders that will keep us spiraling downward until we come to the place where we call out to Him. The evil one will use these leaders and a metaphorical cloud of deception will be placed upon the people. Some will begin to see the error of trusting the leader, while others will continue to be deceived. Would it not be wise to pray for the leader and for this cloud of deception to be lifted?

The Creator is our father. He loves as well as discipline. Sometimes we may not understand why bad things happen to us in our lives. Maybe we should start looking at ourselves and see where we went wrong. We all will be judged at some point. Good or bad, it doesn't matter. It doesn't change the outcome. Why not be a repentant nation rather than one that continues to turn away from the Creator?

We are no longer the true Superpower of the world. The exalted has been brought down low. It is because we have become a den of thieves, a place of harlots, a nation hell-bent on destruction. Do not cry out to the Creator asking why we have been brought down so low. We have done this to ourselves. Is it not time to do an "about face" and begin walking in the right direction?

What is Behind the Curtain

If we now find that for years, possibly centuries, there are things that once were hidden, that now are being revealed, get us to suddenly question everything. What is fact from fiction, in ALL things.

Knowing that, and questioning things now, how can we really continue to move forward in the same frame of mind? We are in a time where everything must be questioned, and we certainly should find out what the truth really is. The scriptures tell us that what had been hidden will ultimately be made manifest. Well, we are at that time now.

Speaking of scriptures, maybe it is time to question why some things were taken out by man, and for what reason. Is it in the best interest to rely solely on one translation, or would it be best to find out the earliest translation from the Hebrew? Keep in mind the names on the first four books of the New Testament were unknown at the time of Jesus. Matthew, Mark, Luke, and John were not Jewish names. So, maybe we ought to question who made up those names and why. Just a thought.

I, for one, have several versions of scriptures, and recently added one called the Cepher (Book or Scroll) which is translated from Hebrew to English. There are passages that are missing from the other versions. But I digress.

If we have been misled, or lied to, by certain parties over the centuries, then we all ought to come to a decision. Do we continue to believe everything we were taught by others, or do we seek out the truth for ourselves? How much has been hidden from us that is available, but has been kept secret for monetary and power means? Why is it that those things we were taught in school, are no longer applicable today? If you believe what you see is trustworthy, then I question your belief system. Why? Because I know for a fact that all is not what it seems. There has been far too much that has been hidden that proves there are far more nefarious things going on, and history isn't as factual as we were taught.

When is It Time to Speak Up

Calvin Coolidge, the 30th president of the United States, was popularly known as "Silent Cal." One time at a party, a woman walked up to him and said, "My husband bet me I couldn't get three words out of you."

Coolidge replied, "You lose."

There are times where it may be best to keep silent. There is an old Native American proverb, that generally goes unheeded, which states "there is strength in silence." Yet there will be times when the Creator expects us to rise up and bring that gift of wisdom into play. We can't always sit back passively, and watch things deteriorate. We can't go through life always wanting to please man. Lord, I know that's true. How often is it that we attempt that, but it ends up biting us in the end? Instead, we should be pleasing the Creator. If we continue to sit back and do nothing, we are not doing the will of the Father. We cannot bring balance to the world if all we are doing is watching from the sidelines. We must be active in our praying and actions. Remember, faith without works is dead.

In this current topsy-turvy world, we ought not completely immerse ourselves into the ways of man. Would it not be better to find knowledge and wisdom in the scriptures and the spirit to combat the evil that surrounds us? We cannot invite hate into our hearts when people are crying out for love. Are we to be like those that do not believe in the saving grace of our Lord? We MUST be a voice of reason. Study, know, and understand what has been written in His Word. Put on that full armor of the Creator. Be silent until you know with certainty what He wants us to do and say at any passing moment.

Quotes from the Author

If a country is to be corruption free and become a nation of beautiful minds, we must be more responsible as fathers, mothers, and teachers.

The most common trait of all indigenous people is a spiritual reverence for the life-giving earth.

Thinking for oneself first will always prevent buyer's remorse. Read the instructions, ingredients, and/or policies and ask yourself if that is what you need.

Normal is a word for comparison. Each person is unique and stands alone. It is not possible for anyone to be rightfully compared to another.

Mother Earth holds healing properties. You will find that those children allowed to play in the dirt are also the healthier ones. Their immune systems are being strengthened by the dirt and mud they play in. So, forget about how dirty they get, let them play! Let the children be children. We can always clean their clothes and themselves later.

With free will there is responsibility. Use your discernment. Choose wisely. Believe it or not believe it, the choice is only yours to make.

One thing needs to be made clear. There is nothing wrong with being successful in business. Much depends on where the focus lies. If it is merely just gaining wealth or harming others, then in my humble opinion, it is evil. If you're gaining wealth but your focus is on helping others, then it isn't. One is of the light; the other is of the dark.

The strongest motivator is not the spoken word but the action itself.

The earth is a living organism that heals. It is very important that we ground ourselves to her as much as possible.

www.ingramcontent.com/pod-product-compliance
Lightning Source LLC
Chambersburg PA
CBHW031302060726
47590CB00003B/1028